PROFESSIONAL ETHICS IN EDUCATION SERIES

The Ethics of
School Administration

Kenneth A. Strike
Emil J. Haller
Jonas F. Soltis

TEACHERS
COLLEGE
PRESS

Teachers College, Columbia University
New York and London

Published by Teachers College Press, 1234 Amsterdam Avenue,
New York, NY 10027

Library of Congress Cataloging-in-Publication Data

Strike, Kenneth A.
  The ethics of school administration.

  (Ethics in education series)
  Bibliography: p.
  Includes index.
  1. School management and organization – United States –
Case studies. 2. School administrators – United States –
Professional ethics – Case studies. I. Haller, Emil J.
II. Soltis, Jonas F. III. Title. IV. Series.
  LB2806.S73 1988   371.2'00973   87-26740

ISBN 0-8077-2887-X

BK
$ 19.50

Manufactured in the United States of America

93 92 91 90   2 3 4 5 6

Contents

Preface

This is the first book in a new Teachers College Press series, Professional Ethics in Education, which is devoted to the examination of ethical issues in all educational settings. The books that will be published as part of this series divide into three distinct groups, as follows.

The first group is intended to teach some central concepts of professional ethics to practitioners. These books will be built around case studies and will focus on helping practitioners to acquire or refine some of the concepts that are crucial in reflecting on ethical issues. These books will be brief and practically oriented. The current volume, *The Ethics of School Administration*, is part of this group.

The second group will focus on pedagogical and curricular issues related to professional ethics. Intended to help in thinking through an approach to teaching about professional ethics, books in this group will pay special attention to the needs of those who are not formally trained in ethics as they strive to work out successful teaching strategies. Since it is our belief that the study of professional ethics should be diffused throughout the curriculum, we feel that books in this part of the series should be of value to all who are involved in the training of educational practitioners.

The third group of books will deal with issues of professional ethics in a rigorous and scholarly way. These books will be topical, treating current controversial issues in order to advance our knowledge and understanding of specific problems. They should be of interest both to scholars and to practitioners who want the opportunity to think through a particular issue thoroughly.

All of the books in this series will aim at helping educators and the education profession to examine and reflect on the ethical issues and controversies that are a normal and routine part of educational practice. We believe that this is an especially important task as education seeks to mold itself more on the model of a self-governing profession. Our world is not one in which eternal verities or the moral sentiments of a cohesive community can easily govern conduct in public institutions. Educators who wish to be responsible for the practice of education must therefore be equipped to take individual responsibility for thinking through defensible positions on difficult ethical questions. We hope to assist in that endeavor.

The present volume, *The Ethics of School Administration*, is intended to help teach a range of ethical concepts that are important to the practicing administrator. Its ample case studies and detailed analyses should provide practitioners with information and skills needed for a knowledgeable approach to thinking through the ethical problems they encounter in the course of their work.

The Ethics of School Administration is largely modeled on Strike and Soltis, *The Ethics of Teaching*, which is part of the Teachers College Press Thinking About Education Series. The editor of that series, Jonas F. Soltis, is also one of the co-authors of this book. We have found the format of the books in the Thinking About Education Series to be quite effective in teaching and have modified it only slightly here, largely by expanding the case material and organizing it topically. Readers who appreciate the content and approach of *The Ethics of School Administration* will also enjoy *The Ethics of Teaching* and the other books in the Thinking About Education Series.

We gratefully acknowledge all of the assistance that led to the current volume. Teachers College Press encouraged the development of both this book and the new series that it introduces. Bernice Oltz typed and edited various portions of the text and brought together numerous other data files to produce this manuscript, doing so with her usual skill, patience, and enthusiasm. A number of students have helped with this book. Pam Ellis and Scott Bilow read it carefully and provided insightful comments. We also profited from discussions with the members of ED 772: Seminar on Professional Ethics. Finally, we have field-tested many of these cases on numerous students whose reactions and feedback have been helpful. To all of these individuals, our sincerest thanks.

Kenneth A. Strike
Editor, Professional Ethics in Education Series

A Note to the Instructor

The purpose of this book is to teach some ethical concepts that are important to educational administration as well as something of the process of ethical reasoning. To this end we have built the book around cases. We believe that ethical reasoning is a skill and that its acquisition requires practice. It is not enough merely to have students read the text. We believe that it is important that cases be thoroughly discussed in class, and we think that it is entirely in order that writing assignments be built around them as well.

We have provided a generous selection of cases that may be used for these purposes. Each substantive chapter begins with a case that is referred to throughout the chapter. Each chapter concludes with several other cases dealing with the issues of that chapter. Finally, at the end of the book we have provided a set of additional cases that are not linked to the topics of specific chapters and that deal with a wide range of ethical issues.

We have tried to construct these cases so that they contain genuine moral dilemmas. Thus it will not be apparent, at the outset, that there is a clearly right response to the case. For this reason they should make good material for discussion.

We believe, however, that it is important that these discussions have a certain character. And we believe that the instructor is vitally important to the effective use of cases. Students are often inclined to approach ambiguous cases by simply stating what they feel should be done. When other students produce different responses, they are apt to conclude that the matter is unresolvable and that everyone is entitled to his or her own opinion. We have also found that the first time around students will frequently miss much of what is at stake in the case.

It is therefore important that students be encouraged to formulate the moral principles that underlie their initial reactions to these cases and that these principles be subject to criticism. It is the process of judging cases against principles and of criticizing and reformulating moral principles that constitutes the art of moral reflection. This is the way students are going to become capable of sophisticated moral reasoning.

The role of the instructor in using these cases is thus Socratic. It consists in drawing out responses from students. But it also consists in criticizing students' initial responses and helping them to formulate views that are more adequate and more thoroughly considered. This book contains an account of the process of ethical reasoning. It is equally an account of how ethical issues can be profitably discussed and argued about. It should provide the instructor with a useful account of what a fruitful classroom discussion is like. Finally, the role of the instructor consists in establishing a classroom climate in which everyone feels free to participate in the process of criticism and debate.

The Ethics of School Administration

CHAPTER 1

Administration and Ethical Thinking

A CASE

Janet Russel, the principal of Haven Elementary School, sat staring out the window. It was a pleasant late spring day. A pair of robins had built a nest in a tree a few feet away, and she could see them darting in and out with an occasional worm or grub. She would have liked to see if the babies were observable from a vantage point closer to the window. But she would have to wait to investigate later.

The feathered domestic tranquility outside provided counterpoint to the absence of tranquility inside. Mr. and Mrs. Taylor were still talking, but Ms. Russel was only half listening. Great attention was not required. She had heard it several times already this week. In fact, she heard it every year at this time. Each spring after the class assignments for next year went home, parents, moved by some primordial urge to secure any marginal advantage for their children, began to migrate toward the school, twittering in frenzied agitation about the placement of their fledglings.

The usual speech went like this: "We know, Ms. Russel, that you work hard to match students to teachers. In the past we have appreciated your attention to the special needs of our child. But this year we think you are wrong. We know our child better than you, and we are sure that our child will do much better with Ms. Tarkington than with Mr. Booth. We would appreciate it if you would make the change."

The first speech was usually polite and tactful. But any resistance escalated matters to a more stressful level. There was the friends-in-high-places ploy. It was hard to believe that school board members and the superintendent of schools had so many personal friends. And of course there were the parents-have-rights and the unresponsive-school-administrators ploys.

The problem was that every parent was right. Their child *would* do better with Ms. Tarkington than with Mr. Booth. Ms. Tarkington was the local superteacher. Children blossomed in her class. Mr. Booth, on the other hand, was—well—undistinguished. Both teachers had reputations in the community. Parents knew.

What could Ms. Russel say? She could not admit that one teacher was far superior to the other. Principals did not do that. She had to be supportive of all her staff. Parents understood that intuitively. Nobody ever came in and said, "I want the best teacher for my child." Euphemisms were the order of the day. After much evasion the parents would leave with her promise to think it over.

She had already thought it over. Obviously she could not simply put every child whose parents requested it in Ms. Tarkington's class. Having one class of 35 children and another of 15 would be noticed. Nor could she move enough children out of Ms. Tarkington's class to compensate for the children transferred in. That would be unfair. It would give an advantage to those children whose parents were willing to come in and lobby on their behalf. It was not surprising that these were usually the parents of middle-class children, who tended to be the most successful in school. To grant parental wishes would be to segregate the class on socioeconomic lines and to systematically assign the least able children to the poorest teacher. Given a choice, Ms. Russel would prefer to do the opposite. Yet she had to grant that parents did have a right to some say about the education of their children. She always listened to their requests, and she granted them whenever she could. But she did not think she ought to do so in this case. Parents' rights or not, it just was not fair.

PURPOSES OF THIS BOOK

Ms. Russel has a problem. It is not just an administrative problem; it is also a moral dilemma regarding a clash between rights and fairness. What makes some administrative problems ethical ones, and how can administrators reach justifiable decisions about moral matters? Asking these question raises others. How do ethical questions differ from factual questions? What is moral or ethical decision making like? Is ethical reasoning really possible? Are not our moral values merely matters of personal choice? Are they not relative to our culture? Can there be objective answers to ethical questions? If so, how do we decide such questions?

In this book we will deal with these basic philosophical questions in the practical context of educational administration. We have a number of objectives in doing so. First, we want to persuade you that objective ethical reasoning is both possible and important for educational administrators. Ethical decisions are not just matters of personal preference. Deciding how to place children, given two teachers of differing ability, is not a matter of taste, like deciding whether to have ice cream or chocolate cake. Instead, we will show you that it is possible to make ethical decisions based on good reasons that others can accept even if such decisions go against their preferences.

In saying that objective ethical reasoning is possible, however, we do not mean to claim that there is always one right answer to every moral dilemma. Ethical situations often require that hard choices be made under complex and ambiguous circumstances. It is difficult to be sure that we have made a good decision. At the same time, one choice is often better than another. In the case above, for example, Ms. Russel believes that it is morally better to assign children to classes fairly, rather than to concede to parents the right of choice. We agree with her. We also believe that it is possible to give reasons for our choices, to decide objectively on the basis of these reasons, and to persuade others who are willing to judge our evidence fairly that our views are correct. If we are open-minded and reasonable people, we must also grant that sometimes we will be persuaded to change our own minds. Moral reasoning has a moral point, and it can help us to make better and more justified moral decisions if we see the moral point. Ms. Russel seems to sense the importance of morally justifying her acts. At least her comment that "it just wasn't fair" suggests that she does. But "it just wasn't fair" is not much of a justification. As a professional, she needs to be able to specify what being fair means in this context, and she needs to be able to articulate her reasons to others.

Therefore, another of our major purposes in this book is to help you learn how to engage in ethical reflection and justification. Not that you do not already know how. After all, people engage in ethical reflection all the time. But we do think that we can help you to do it better. Part of our task will be to sensitize you to the kinds of moral issues that arise in the normal activities of administrative life. That is one of the reasons we will use cases extensively in this book. We also believe that we can help you to state some ethical principles and arguments more clearly and bring them to bear on your own decisions where principles conflict in actual situations. As a consequence, we expect that you will be a better administrator.

THE NATURE OF ETHICAL INQUIRY

What makes Ms. Russel's administrative problem a *moral* dilemma? We are going to talk about the characteristics of moral issues in more detail in the next chapter, but let us make a start here. Ms. Russel's dilemma has the following characteristics. First, it concerns what is the *right* thing to do, not just the most expedient or least trouble making, but the *fair* or *just* thing. Moral issues are usually characterized by certain kinds of language. Words such as *right, ought, just,* and *fair* are common. Moral issues concern our duties and obligations to one another, what constitutes just or fair treatment of one another, and what rights we each have.

Second, Ms. Russel's dilemma cannot be settled by the facts. Facts are relevant in deciding moral questions, but they are not sufficient in deciding them. Ms. Russel knows what the consequences of her choices will be. She knows that if she fulfills parental assignment requests, those children who have less aggressive parents or who are less academically able will end up with the poorer teacher. But that does not solve her moral problem. It does not tell her what is a fair way to assign students to teachers. Nor does it tell her what rights parents should have in the education of their children. The facts here are insufficient to allow her to decide. She also needs to bring some moral principles—principles about fairness and rights—to bear on her decision.

Finally, Ms. Russel finds herself in a moral dilemma because her moral sentiments conflict. This is a typical characteristic. She has appealed intuitively to two moral principles at the same time, although she has not stated either with much clarity. On one hand, she has appealed to a principle of fairness. It is not fair for the weakest students to have the poorest teacher. On the other hand, she has recognized the principle of parents' rights. Parents do have a right to a say about the education of their children. Even without further clarification of these principles, given the facts of the case, it is apparent that they conflict. To resolve her dilemma, Ms. Russel needs to be clearer about these two principles and how they are justified. She also would have to have some idea about the priorities of such principles when they conflict.

These characteristics of Ms. Russel's dilemma suggest some of the general features of ethical reasoning. One part of ethical reasoning is the application of principles to cases. Applying moral principles to cases requires expressing and clarifying the principles and finding out the relevant facts about the cases. For example, the principle of fairness to which Ms. Russel is appealing might be based on the idea of equality of educational opportunity. This would mean that the educational resources made available to children should not depend on such irrelevant characteristics as family background, race, or socioeconomic class. Once we understand the facts of the case, however, we find that these would be the deciding characteristics if Ms. Russel granted parental requests for the assignment of their children to teachers. Middle-class children would end up with the better teachers.

In order to perform this task of aptly applying principles to facts, we may also have to inquire into the justification of the principle. This is another aspect of ethical reasoning. Why should we accept the principle of equality of educational opportunity? What purposes does it serve? We may not be able to understand the exact nature of its application until we have a clear idea of its point and rationale.

Often, in thinking about these questions, we are led to ask further questions of a different and more complex sort. How should we decide between conflicting ethical principles? How in general do we justify ethical principles? What is the nature of moral evidence? How do we distinguish moral from nonmoral claims? And can we construct a general ethical theory that orders our ethical principles under some general view of the Good Life?

The differences among these ethical questions is not sharp. They seem easily to lead into one another. Nevertheless, they do seem to differ in roughly the following way. One set of questions (i.e., how to apply the principle of equal opportunity) seems directly concerned with what we ought to do in a specific situation. We want to know how we should act and why we should act that way, here and now, in these circumstances. The concern is for the morally correct choice and its justification in a specific context. The next set of questions (i.e., how to resolve conflicts between ethical principles) seems to be more general. They are about our process of moral reasoning itself. Here we need to describe our process of justification and to understand how it is possible for us to engage in productive ethical reflection in any situation. We are not so much concerned with the justification of particular actions as with the justification of our moral principles and our ethical theories. We seek to locate our particular moral principles in a general view of the moral life that orders our principles and tells us how to decide when they conflict.

Philosophers often mark the difference between these concerns by calling the first set *ethical* questions and the second set *meta-ethical* questions. We are not going to use those terms after this chapter, but the two sorts of questions are reflected in the structure of this book. In each of the next five chapters you will find four sections, two dealing with ethical issues and two with meta-ethical issues. First there will be a "Case" that, like the case of Ms. Russel in this chapter, sets up the ethical dilemma. Next there will be an imaginary "Dispute" that lays out some of the ethical issues in the case in an intuitive way. Disputes will be similar to the kinds of discussions that occur in a dorm room or in a teachers' lounge when people sense something is morally amiss and argue over what is ethically problematic. Next will come a discussion of the particular ethical "Concepts" that are important to thinking about the meta-ethical issues of the case. In these discussions, we will explore the meaning and justification of such principles as liberty, equality, and due process. Finally, in a section headed "Analysis," will come a meta-ethical discussion of the general features of moral reasoning and moral theories. Each chapter ends with some additional cases and questions for your further reflection on the major concepts treated in the chapter.

LEARNING MORAL REASONING

We have adopted this organization because of our convictions about how people can learn moral reasoning. We use cases because part of the process of moral reflection is learning how to apply principles to real problems. Part of learning to think is learning to see the world through useful concepts. We employ disputes because we believe that your intuitive moral reactions, your feelings about what is right and wrong, and your initial attempts to describe the principles that underlie your feelings are an important initial source of moral data. Much of ethical reasoning is an attempt to state and test systematically and accurately the principles that underlie one's "gut" reactions. In the section called "Concepts," we will discuss such educationally important concepts as intellectual and personal liberty, equality, due process, and democracy. What do they mean? Why should we accept them as principles to guide ethical decision making? These discussions get at the substance of ethical reasoning but also raise some meta-ethical issues. Finally, in the section titled "Analysis," we will raise a number of other meta-ethical issues. These issues are important for understanding how ethical reasoning progresses. We raise them because it has been our experience as teachers of professional ethics that it is impossible to get very far with a discussion of an ethical question before these issues become important. In our classrooms, questions such as "Isn't that just your personal opinion?" or "Aren't you trying to impose your values on us?" occur during the first hour. (They are probably thought of during the first minute.) If we are to help people think constructively about ethical issues, we will have to help them think about such meta-ethical issues as well.

Ultimately then, the purpose of this book is to help administrators and prospective administrators think through some of the ethical problems they encounter in doing their jobs so that they may become more responsible and ethical as administrators. Our focus will be on some major concepts used by administrators in ethical reasoning and on the process of ethical reflection itself. Human beings are moral agents. They are responsible for their choices, and they have a duty to make choices in a morally responsible way. Thus it is crucial that people be able to reflect ethically on their choices and their actions. This is especially important when individuals have power and influence over the lives of others. We can think of few areas where it is more important than in the administration of schools.

CHAPTER 2

Intellectual Liberty

Paul Robinson, principal of Sutton High, was sitting in a chair in the superintendent's office, but he knew he was really on the carpet. Dr. Higgins was holding a copy of the morning paper. The paper was conspicuously folded to reveal the "Letters to the Editor" section. As Paul knew from his own inspection of the paper at breakfast, the phantom letter writer had struck again.

At least today he wished Eliza Fitzgerald was a phantom. But she was all too real. She had a busy pen, which she frequently employed to inform the good citizens of the district of the alleged foibles of the administrators and teachers of their local schools. Last year it had been the athletic program. Student athletes, in her view, received easy grades to keep them eligible. The year before it had been the English program in the middle school. Why, oh why, she had wondered, did she continue to have to correct the writing of the newly arrived freshmen? If only the middle school teachers were as competent as she.

Needless to say, she was not an especially popular figure at the middle school. Perhaps her comments were resented because they were usually true. Ms. Fitzgerald was not only the district's most noteworthy character, she was also its foremost English teacher. Numbered among her students were several newspaper editors and an award-winning novelist. Students returning to class reunions spent a great deal of time rehearsing Fitzgerald stories. She was a legend of sorts. Students wore her dressing-downs and her D – grades like purple hearts. They were proud of the sarcasm and abuse she had heaped on their sentence fragments and mangled paragraphs. And they knew she cared for them.

This year she had elected to go after big fish. The district was in the process of negotiating a new contract. Negotiations were at a crucial and sensitive phase. Moreover, the relations between administrators and teachers had become strained. The teachers had initiated a job action and were "working to rule" – doing the minimum their contract required. Administrators had responded by tightening up on the rules teachers worked to. Teachers had to show up on time and dared not leave early. Lesson plans were checked carefully and were frequently returned for correction. The air was filled with technicalities and litigiousness.

Ms. Fitzgerald was distraught about the effect this tense atmosphere was having on the education of "her" students and on the welfare of "her" school. Her response was a literary hand grenade to the local paper that scattered verbal shrapnel at everyone in sight. She had devoted special attention to Dr. Higgins and the union representative, Mr. Twist, comparing one to Shylock and the other to Silas Marner. For those who missed the literary allusions, she had left little doubt that she believed that the love of money was the root of a great evil in the district. Teachers and administrators had sold their birthright as educators to squabble over a mess of pottage.

Dr. Higgins might have triumphed over the allusion to Shylock. Indeed, it seemed that he had only a vague notion of who Shylock was. But he cared greatly for the success of the negotiations, and he was most apprehensive about the possibility that Ms. Fitzgerald's letter would make them more difficult. Moreover, Ms. Fitzgerald had weakened her case in Dr. Higgins's eyes by allowing a widespread rumor about the negotiations to creep into her letter. She had helped spread the idea that the district was insisting on a merit-pay provision in the contract. Dr. Higgins had, of course, talked about merit pay to some community groups. Indeed, this was a ploy on his part to secure a higher level of cooperation from the union. But, in fact, the district had made no such proposal to the union. Thus, Ms. Fitzgerald had allowed an error to spoil her legendary reputation for getting it right. Dr. Higgins was livid.

He had a simple suggestion. Paul Robinson was to tell Ms. Fitzgerald to shut up. Any further letters on the topic would be regarded by the district as insubordination, and Ms. Fitzgerald would be dealt with accordingly.

Paul had grave reservations about saying this to Ms. Fitzgerald. It would only make her worse, and he had considerable doubt as to who would end up dealing with whom. It did not pay to underrate Ms. Fitzgerald. Moreover, Paul had vague recollections from his undergraduate days that notions such as free speech and a free press were important in our society. He wondered if the attorney whom the district kept on retainer had earned his fee lately. But Dr. Higgins was not in a mood to be reasonable. He wanted Ms. Fitzgerald silenced and was not taking "no" for an answer. Thus, Paul lifted himself from Dr. Higgins's carpet and started back to his office to call Ms. Fitzgerald onto his. He had few illusions about his ability to keep her there.

DISPUTE

A: People have a right, a basic right, to speak their piece no matter what. That is what freedom of speech means in our society.

B: No, it doesn't. You can't publicly say false and malicious things about people. That's libel. And in the United States, you can't preach violent overthrow of the government. That's sedition. Even in a democratic society, there have to be some constraints on free speech.

A: Oh, I don't mean those things; I mean freedom to state your opinion even if it is disagreeable to those in authority.

B: But what if your opinion is wrong and contains falsehoods or is just plain stupid?

A: As judged by whom? That's the whole point. Opinions and ideas can't be censored or suppressed in a free society. There has to be the presumption that the truth will win out only if there is free competition among ideas.

B: That sounds great in theory, but what if your personal opinion is harmful to the welfare of others?

A: How can opinions hurt people? That's ridiculous!

B: No, it isn't. Suppose you are someone in authority, a policeman or a teacher, say. Suppose, in your opinion, people from a certain ethnic group are stupid, crafty, and dishonest. Don't tell me you wouldn't treat them differently!

A: Sure, you might, but just *saying* they are "stupid, crafty, and dishonest" isn't harmful. It is only harmful when you act on your beliefs. It is important to see that we are talking about free speech, not about actions Acts can be harmful, not words.

B: I'm not sure that just saying things like that about people isn't harmful. If I were the police commissioner or the superintendent of schools, I'd make a rule against the use of derogatory language regarding any ethnic group by my staff, wouldn't you?

A: No. There can never be a good reason to constrain free speech.

B: Then what about libel and sedition?

CONCEPT: FREEDOM OF EXPRESSION

Dr. Higgins and Paul Robinson are about to challenge Ms. Fitzgerald's right to express her views about school district matters to the public. Dr. Higgins believes he has good reason to do this, that it is necessary in order to permit the negotiations between the district and the union to go smoothly. He is doing it for the good of the district. The sooner the negotiations are settled, the sooner everyone can get back to running the schools and teaching students. Everyone will be better off.

Will everyone be better off? Is this a sufficient reason to threaten Ms. Fitzgerald with disciplinary action should she write another letter? The issue is one of intellectual freedom. In a free society people are supposed to be free to hold their own opinions and to express them. But why should this be their right, and what are the limits on a person's right to express his or her views?

At the outset, it is important to distinguish between the right to hold an opinion and the right to express it. Generally, we may assume that the right to believe what one wants is absolute. No one has a right to tell us what we may believe. Part of the reason for this is that beliefs do not have consequences for people, other than those who hold them, so long as they are not expressed or acted upon. But to say or to write something is to act. So actions based on our beliefs may have consequences for the welfare of others. Thus the freedom to act on our opinions and beliefs cannot be absolute. We must inquire into its limits.

Note that in these comments we have already made some important ethical assumptions. We have assumed that people have a right to be the authors of their own beliefs. Why assume this? And we have assumed that a person's actions can be regulated only when they injure the welfare of others. Is this correct, and why should we believe it?

It does seem that the harmfulness of some speech acts can be a reason for limiting freedom of expression. Supreme Court Justice Oliver Wendell Holmes wrote that the right to free speech does not give one the right to yell "fire!" in a crowded theater. It seems reasonable, then, that if the immediate consequence of some expression of opinion is that the lives and property of others will be endangered, then that is a good reason to forbid it.

On the other hand, the view that the expression of ideas can be restricted because some harm might result seems quite dangerous to the values of free speech and a free press. Often people believe that the views of those who disagree with them are dangerous and harmful. Indeed, some ideas *are* dangerous and harmful. For example, the belief that the members of some races or religions are inherently inferior has been and continues to be a cause of much human suffering. But if we are willing to repress ideas simply because they are potentially harmful, we will do great violence to freedom of expression. Politicians often believe that the views of their opponents are dangerous and harmful. If potential harm or danger is allowed as a good reason for repressing speech, free and open debate about matters of public policy will soon disappear. Indeed, if Dr. Higgins's opinion that Ms. Fitzgerald's letter will harm negotiations were to count as a good reason for suppressing her right to express her views on matters of educational policy, then we would not need to inquire further to decide the issue raised in the case. It is true that Ms. Fitzgerald has endangered sensitive negotiations. Her letter may perpetuate the unpleasant tensions in the schools and damage the educational process. What more do we need to know?

We hope you will agree that we do need to know more. The fact that an idea is harmful or that someone believes that it is harmful is not a sufficient reason to forbid its expression. If we believe otherwise, we will end up eliminating free discussion about very many issues, especially those that are most important.

Why should we so value free expression? What is its point and justifica
tion? To address these questions, we should consider some classical arguments
for freedom found in John Stuart Mill's essay, "On Liberty."

> First, if any opinion is compelled to silence, that opinion may, for aught we
> can certainly know, be true. To deny this is to assume our own infallibility.
>   Secondly, though the silenced opinion may be an error, it may and very
> often does, contain a portion of the truth; and since the general or prevailing
> opinion on any subject is rarely or never the whole truth, it is only by the
> collision of adverse opinions that the remainder of the truth has any chance
> of being supplied.
>   Thirdly, even if the received opinion be not only true, but the whole
> truth, unless it is suffered to be, and actually is rigorously and earnestly
> contested, it will, by most of those who receive it, be held in the manner of a
> prejudice, with little comprehension of its rational grounds. And not only
> this, but fourthly, the meaning of the doctrine itself will be in danger of
> becoming lost or enfeebled, and deprived of its virtual effect on the character
> and conduct; the dogma becoming a mere formal profession, inefficacious for
> good, but cumbering the ground and preventing the growth of any real and
> heartfelt conviction from reason and personal experience. (Mill, 1859/1956,
> p. 64)

Here Mill provides us with some of the more powerful arguments for free
expression. Free expression is a condition of inquiry and the discovery of the
truth. We can never refine or improve our ideas if we do not permit them to be
challenged. Ideas are tested in debate. Truth is best sought by a process of
criticism and debate. Not only that, but if our ideas are not contested we soon
lose sight of why we held them and, eventually, of their full meaning. Untested
ideas degenerate into platitudes and clichés and cease to affect action.

We might consider the case of Ms. Fitzgerald in the light of Mill's arguments. Educational policy in our society is made democratically. Members of
school boards and state legislators, those who make most educational policy,
are elected. How are voters to vote intelligently about matters of educational
policy without information? And how can they refine their thinking about
matters of educational policy unless educational issues are debated? Moreover,
who is better placed to inform the public about educational issues than teachers? One might argue, then, that Ms. Fitzgerald has performed a public service
by informing the public of her views on a matter of interest to them. She has
generated debate and discussion on an important matter. Will not the public
be better informed and have a more reasonable view of the issues on her
account? Ms. Fitzgerald is simply exemplifying the process of free and open
debate that Mill so ably argues for, with the results that Mill anticipated.

One reason for protecting the right of free expression, then, is because criticism and debate are conditions of rationality itself. The public store of tested ideas is enlarged, and rational public decision making is improved. We cannot make competent decisions without free expression.

A second reason for valuing freedom is that it promotes personal growth. Here, too, Mill speaks eloquently.

> He who lets the world, or his own portion of it, choose his plan of life for him has no need of any other faculty than the ape-like one of imitation. He who chooses his plan for himself employs all his faculties. He must use observation to see, reasoning and judgment to foresee, activity to gather materials for decision, firmness and self-control to hold to his deliberate decision. And these qualities he requires and exercises exactly in proportion as the part of his conduct which he determines according to judgment and feeling is a large one. (Mill, 1859/1956, pp. 71–72)

Personal growth requires freedom. Participation in the processes of reflection, argument, and deliberation that go into the evaluation of ideas not only improves the ideas, it also enhances the intellectual competence of the participants. Thus, Ms. Fitzgerald not only has informed the public about an important issue, but by stirring up a debate she has contributed to the growth and competence of the participants. Perhaps Dr. Higgins does not now feel greatly improved by Ms. Fitzgerald's letter. But on another day, when the dust has settled, he may be willing to admit that she helped him see how his actions affected students and made him a better superintendent as a consequence.

Freedom of expression thus contributes to the refining of ideas, to competent decision making, and to personal growth. Are these reasons why we should value free expression? It seems self-evident that better ideas, competent decision making, and personal growth are valuable. Nevertheless, our grasp of the reasons for free expression may be enhanced by further exploring the reasons undergirding these values. Let us ask, then, why we should value better ideas, competent decision making, and growth.

One response is that we should value these things because they contribute to the overall welfare of society and its members. If the capacity of society or of individuals to evaluate ideas, make better decisions, and grow is enhanced, we will all be better off. People will make more sensible decisions. More people will get more of what they want. We will all be happier as a result. Thus free speech and a free press are ultimately of value because they contribute to human welfare and human happiness.

Another sort of response is possible. Here the ultimate value to be realized is not happiness, but the realization of individual moral agency. Human beings are free moral agents. This means not only that they are able to make decisions about themselves, but also that they have the responsibility to do so. When people are responsible for their choices, they have a duty to make their choices wisely.

Now, if I have a duty as a moral agent to make responsible choices, I also have an interest in the availability of the resources that will enable me to choose wisely. Other human beings, as moral agents, also have this interest. Insofar as we are obligated to respect one another's status as moral agents, this is an interest that we each must respect. This means that I and others have a right to necessary information. It may also mean that I have a right to expect that I can freely discuss ideas with others or benefit from the discussions and debates of others. If I am to make competent choices, I will need the best ideas and information I can obtain. If free speech, a free press, and freedom of information are important in making ideas available to me, then, as a moral agent, I have a right to these things. Finally, as a moral agent, I have a right to the conditions that make it possible for me to evaluate and choose between competing ideas. One of these conditions is the free and open debate of ideas. Another is an education that teaches such evaluative skills.

From the perspective of this argument, we may wish to claim that Ms. Fitzgerald has done a service to the voters of her district, who are eventually to be faced with the need to make a responsible choice as to whom they will support in school board elections or as to what policies they will advocate. She has helped them to be more responsible in fulfilling their civic duties.

Both of these arguments make a strong case for such institutions as free speech, a free press, and freedom of information. The first argument emphasizes the social utility of these institutions. The second emphasizes their importance to the individual faced with the moral requirement to make responsible choices. Ms. Fitzgerald may have served both of these purposes.

Is this a sufficient case for Ms. Fitzgerald? Shall we conclude that she has or should have a right to write her letters to the editor and that it is improper for Dr. Higgins or Paul Robinson to attempt to stop her? At this point such a conclusion would be premature. We must also consider whether there are other rights or interests that conflict with Ms. Fitzgerald's freedom to write her letters.

Dr. Higgins is sure to argue that there is an important right that conflicts with Ms. Fitzgerald's right to take advantage of the free press. There are sensitive negotiations in progress. Ms. Fitzgerald's letter may have an adverse effect on these negotiations. If negotiations break down and teachers strike, would not the students' right to an education suffer? Is this not a sufficient reason to curtail Ms. Fitzgerald's literary excesses? Moreover, her letter contained some factual errors. Does the right of a free press include the right to be wrong? Can Ms. Fitzgerald be allowed to jeopardize the negotiations with her mistakes? We are not going to consider these issues in depth, but we do have two observations on them.

First, we believe that rights, in general, are not absolute. Often they can conflict with other rights or with other important interests. In this case, Ms. Fitzgerald's ideas and her letter may well have adverse consequences for the negotiations, and, if the negotiations are harmed and the tensions between administrators and teachers continue, the children of the district may have their right to an education infringed upon. We must, then, address the question of how to balance the right of intellectual freedom against other rights and interests.

Second, however, we must also insist that intellectual freedom is a most important right in our society. We have already stated the basic arguments for it. It serves important considerations of social utility and individual responsibility. Thus, if there are other considerations that may be balanced against it and that are sufficiently weighty to tip the scales against free speech or a free press, they must be very weighty indeed. Are there such weighty considerations in favor of suppressing Ms. Fitzgerald?

ANALYSIS: ETHICAL DECISION MAKING

What do educational administrators do? How would one characterize their role? Obviously there is no one answer to these questions. Administrators are decision makers. They are leaders. They are organizers. They facilitate the work of faculty. They make up budgets, hire and evaluate teachers, and allocate resources. They deal with students, parents, and school boards.

Many, perhaps all, of these administrative tasks involve an ethical component. If the administrator is a leader or a decision maker, questions arise as to whether decisions are made fairly or democratically. If administrators allocate resources, they must do so justly and equitably. If they evaluate teachers, they must do so fairly and humanely. If they discipline students, their punishments must be just. Note the words: *just, fair, equitable, humane.* Ethics seems to be part of the job. Administrators who are seen as unfair, unjust, inhumane, or capricious in their decisions usually buy themselves a great deal of trouble in their jobs. Indeed, it has been our experience that administrators are just as likely to fail because they are seen as unjust as they are to fail because they are seen as inefficient. The administrator who is unfair will soon be faced with a hostile faculty and an angry community. Ethics *is* part of the job. Indeed, it is an essential part of the job. Administrators deal with fairness, equality, justice, and democracy as much as they deal with test scores, teachers' salaries, parents, and budgets.

If this is so, then it is surprising that few universities offer courses on administrative ethics. If ethics is part of the job, why is ethical decision making not a part of the training of school administrators? One response to this question might be that administration is a science and so should not deal with values. As for decision making, the best guide to our actions, so the argument goes, is well-confirmed scientific research that connects actions with their consequences. Boards and the public determine ends, educators the means to achieve the desired ends. It is science that tells us what decisions and actions will bring about policies and goals deemed by others to be desirable. This seems to be the view of administration that is assumed in many of the leading textbooks.

Perhaps so. Yet the science of administration, if there is one, still seems insufficient. It is not clear that any amount of scientific inquiry can tell us whether an evaluation is fair, whether a decision is democratic, or whether some allocation of resources is equitable. Indeed, sometimes we can know what the consequences of our actions will be but not know if the action itself is right. A moral residue seems to be left. We need to make moral as well as management judgments.

But moral judgments are value judgments! How can we learn how to make them correctly? Often the phrase "that's a value judgment" is used to halt conversations. It appears to mean that the matter in question is something about which there is no right or wrong answer. It is all just a matter of opinion. It depends on our tastes or our feelings. Thus there is no point in talking about it further. No rational resolution of value issues is possible.

If this were true, it would explain why ethics is not a part of the study of administration. There is nothing to study; that is, there is no relevant body of knowledge. There is only how people happen to feel or what they happen to believe is right or wrong. There is nothing to be learned and known. We might, of course, scientifically study what people believe about what is right or wrong, and this might help us deal with them more successfully, but there is no method of inquiry suitable for determining whether any ethical view or decision really is correct.

Is this true? One of the purposes of this book is to persuade you that it is not. Part of the problem, we think, is the sloppy use of such phrases as "value judgment." We think that moral claims are not value judgments in the sense of being only personal or group preferences. But that is a topic for the next chapter. Here we should note that in the "Concepts" section of this chapter we seemed perfectly capable of producing objectively compelling reasons for moral claims. We argued that as moral agents and in order to promote social well-being, people *ought* to have a right to intellectual liberty. If you accept that basic argument, then it follows that people are entitled to their own opinions and beliefs and that they are entitled to express them or publish them. Free speech and a free press promote the public welfare and individual responsibility. We also suggested that these rights might need to be balanced against other rights and interests.

All of these claims are moral claims. Moreover, we gave arguments for them. Perhaps you were not persuaded by everything we had to say, but we are willing to bet that it did not seem to you that there was something strange or wrong about the very fact that we were trying to argue for moral claims rather than merely express our preferences or our beliefs. In the real world, when we are not doing philosophical exercises, we all manage to have cogent moral discussions all the time. We give and listen to arguments about what is right or wrong with no suspicion that such matters are simply "value judgments" and thus merely matters of taste.

This suggests a strategy. We propose a working hypothesis, to be tested in the remainder of the book: namely, that moral arguments and moral discussions have a valid function in our lives and in our institutions. That is, we tentatively assert that sometimes it is possible to decide, as a result of hearing arguments and weighing evidence, that some actions are right and others wrong. In other cases that are, perhaps, not so clear, it is still possible to decide that some choices are morally preferable to others. If we accept this working hypothesis that moral discourse has a valid function in reaching ethical decisions, then we can focus on the question of how it is that we can and do successfully discuss moral matters with one another. If we can give a plausible account of how we actually proceed to have meaningful moral discussions, perhaps we will not have to have our conversations stopped by "that's a value judgment."

Let us look more closely at our discussion about Ms. Fitzgerald's right of free expression. How did we argue for that right? We did so by appealing to two different moral principles. On the one hand, we appealed to the good of the public interest. We argued that free expression helps people to make better decisions and that, as a consequence, all people are better off. Second, we appealed to the moral principle of individual responsibility. We said that since people are moral agents and responsible for their choices, they have a right to expect that those conditions that provide for the opportunity of responsible choice will be fulfilled. And we said that the right to information was one such condition. These arguments, in turn, presuppose two even more fundamental moral conceptions. They are *the principle of benefit maximization* and *the principle of equal respect for persons*.

The Principle of Benefit Maximization

The principle of benefit maximization holds that, whenever we are faced with a choice, the best and most just decision is the one that results in the most good or the greatest benefit for the most people. Thus the principle of benefit maximization judges the morality of our actions by their consequences. It says that the best action is the one with the best overall results. It does not directly tell us what is to count as a benefit or a good. That requires additional reflection. It merely says that once we know what is good, the best decision is the one that maximizes good outcomes. If, for example, the production of happiness is thought to be a basic good, then the principle of benefit maximization indicates that we should make those decisions and engage in those actions that result in the greatest happiness for the greatest number. You may have heard this version of the principle of benefit maximization referred to as "utilitarianism."

The Principle of Equal Respect

The principle of equal respect requires that we act in ways that respect the equal worth of moral agents. It requires that we regard human beings as having intrinsic worth and treat them accordingly. The essence of this idea is expressed in the Golden Rule. We have a duty to accord others the same kind of treatment we expect them to accord us. The principle of equal respect can be seen as involving three subsidiary ideas.

First, the principle of equal respect requires us to treat people as *ends rather than means*. This means that we may not treat them as though they were simply means to further our own goals. We must respect their goals as well. We cannot treat people as though they were things, mere objects, who are valued only insofar as they contribute to our welfare. We must consider their welfare as well. People cannot be treated as though they were nothing more than instruments to serve our purposes.

Second, when we are considering what it means to treat people as ends rather than means, we must regard as central the fact that persons are *free and rational moral agents*. This means that, above all, we must respect their freedom of choice. And we must respect the choices people make even when we do not agree with them. Moreover, it means that we must attach a high priority to enabling people to decide responsibly. It is important that people have the information and the education that will enable them to function responsibly as free moral agents.

Third, no matter how people differ, as moral agents they are *of equal value*. This does not mean that we must see people as equal insofar as their abilities or capacities are concerned. Nor does it mean that relevant differences among people cannot be recognized in deciding how to treat them. It is not, for example, a violation of equal respect to pay one person more than another because that person works harder and contributes more. That people are of equal value as moral agents means that they are entitled to the same basic rights and that their interests are of equal value. Everyone, regardless of native ability, is entitled to equal opportunity. Everyone is entitled to one vote in a democratic election, and every vote should be worth the same as every other vote. No one is entitled to act as though his or her happiness counted for more than the happiness of others. As persons, everyone has equal worth.

CONCLUSION

We want you to notice a few important things about the principles of benefit maximization and equal respect. First, we suspect that both principles (in some form) are part of the moral concepts of everyone who is reading this book. These are the sorts of fundamental moral principles that everyone appeals to at some time or another in making moral arguments. We may have formulated them in a way new to you, but the ideas themselves will be familiar. They form part of our common ethical understandings. We appealed to both principles in arguing about freedom of expression. We held that free expression results in more knowledgeable and more competent decisions and that such decisions make everyone better off. This argument appeals to the principle of benefit maximization. We also argued that, as responsible moral agents, people are entitled to the resources that help them to make more competent decisions. This appeals to the principle of equal respect. Both principles were involved in the argument. One, the other, or both seem to appear in most moral arguments. They are part of our everyday ethical thinking.

Second, both principles seem dependent upon each other. Neither is sufficient by itself. The principle of equal respect requires us to value the welfare of other people; that is, we must value their well-being equally to our own and equally to that of others. But to value the welfare of ourselves and of others is to be concerned with benefits. Indeed, it is to be concerned with maximizing benefits. We will want people to be as well off as possible.

Conversely, the principle of benefit maximization seems to presuppose the principle of equal respect. Why, after all, must we value the welfare of others? Why not insist that only our happiness counts, or that our happiness is more important than the happiness of others? Answers to these questions will quickly lead us to affirm that people are of equal worth and that, as a consequence, everyone's happiness is to be valued equally. Thus, our two principles seem intertwined.

Third, however, the principles may also conflict. There are times when it appears that if we are to follow the logic of the principle of benefit maximization, we must violate the principle of equal respect and vice versa. Suppose, for example, that Dr. Higgins is right in that further letters from Ms. Fitzgerald will, in fact, destroy the negotiations and harm the education of the children of the district. The principle of benefit maximization, then, may lead us to the conclusion that Ms. Fitzgerald should be silenced for the good of all. If we are to respect her as a person, however, we must respect her right to express her views even if she might harm the negotiations. To hold otherwise would be to treat her as though she were only a means to the end of the welfare of others.

So even if we are obligated to give each principle its due, sometimes we must decide which is to take precedence. To do that we need to see not only how they are related to each other, but also how they differ. One of the differences between the principle of benefit maximization and the principle of equal respect is the regard they have for the consequences. For the principle of benefit maximization, all that matters is consequences. The sole relevant factor in choosing between courses of action is to decide which action has the best result. But for the principle of equal respect, consequences are not always decisive. What is decisive is that our actions respect the dignity and worth of the individuals involved. We are required to respect people's rights even if in doing so we choose a course that produces less benefit than some other possible action. Thus the crucial question that usually characterizes a conflict between the principle of benefit maximization and the principle of equal respect is this: When is it permissible to violate a person's rights in order to produce a better outcome?

Often philosophers call ethical views that are dominated by the principle of benefit maximization *consequentialist* theories. Such theories rely solely on consequences to judge the morality of an action. By contrast, for *nonconsequentialist* theories, consequences are not decisive. Nonconsequentialists are not oblivious to consequences. However, the crucial thing that makes an action a moral action for the nonconsequentialist who takes as basic the principle of equal respect is that the action taken gives first consideration to the value and dignity of persons. Sometimes this will lead a nonconsequentialist to prefer an action that respects a person's rights over an action that produces the best consequences.

In subsequent chapters, we will show you how consequentialists and nonconsequentialists might reason about the various ethical issues in administration that we shall deal with. We believe that the tension between these two views is a common feature in the kinds of ethical dilemmas administrators face. We also believe that understanding them will help you become a better diagnostician of moral dilemmas and a better ethical decision maker.

ADDITIONAL CASES

Equal Time?

It had seemed like a good idea at the time. Now Dr. Sam Turner wasn't so sure. He had to admit that Mr. Foster of ESTA had a point. Maybe the board of education brochure had been a political statement. But he didn't see why the school district had to provide Foster's antitax group with "equal time" when doing so could very well send the budget vote down in defeat. Why should he assist a group opposed to badly needed improvements in East Salem's schools? As he saw it, his job as the district's superintendent was to improve the education of kids, not make it worse.

This latest town-gown flap, like so many others in East Salem, involved money. The district was a relatively poor one, a condition made worse by recent cuts in state funds. It had to struggle to provide a quality education to its students. Part of that struggle involved convincing district taxpayers that their already high tax rate should be made even higher. If the schools were going to provide a decent computer education program, if they were going to give teachers a much deserved raise, and if they were going to initiate the new math curriculum, money would be required. Sam Turner had worked hard to convince a skeptical board of education that it should propose a 14% tax increase to district voters to cover the costs of these items, as well as to cover the continually rising costs of its regular programs.

The board had gone along with Sam's proposal, though several members were highly dubious of the plan. They pointed out that budget votes in East Salem were always touch and go and seemed to be getting more so. Last year the voters had passed the budget by the slimmest margin yet. Since then, one of the larger manufacturing plants in town had closed. Unemployment was up. It didn't seem like a good time to hit people with a substantial boost in their taxes. One board member thought that they might face a major tax revolt—a revolt that would not only defeat the new initiatives but also make it more difficult to get them approved next year. It might also create serious problems for all future attempts to improve the district's programs. She had pointed out that at present the community's opposition to school improvements and higher taxes was largely unorganized. Asking for 14% might be enough of a catalyst to create a permanent, organized, and powerful opposition. Nevertheless, Sam convinced the board, and the proposed tax increase was announced.

Sam also convinced the board of the need to mount a sustained effort to inform the voters of the wisdom of the increase. As part of that effort, Sam had written a carefully worded brochure describing how the district would use the money and the benefits students would receive as a result. In it he had pointed out, for example, that at present only a very few of the district's pupils had access to a computer and that the new program would give every secondary student a chance to become computer literate—an essential skill in today's world. He had also called attention to the fact that the East Salem salary schedule was the lowest in the region and that the district couldn't expect to attract competent staff at current salaries. The brochure was printed and mailed, at the district's expense, to every voter in town.

Two weeks later Mr. Foster appeared in Sam's office. He was, he said, the president of the newly created East Salem Taxpayers' Association. The association had formed, he explained, to monitor the uses of citizens' tax dollars and to inform community residents of inefficiency, waste, and misuse of their money. Toward that end, the association had prepared a brochure, a copy of which Foster gave to Sam, along with the request that Sam have it printed and mailed to every voter in East Salem—at the district's expense.

Sam was impressed with the association's handiwork. Whoever had written the pamphlet had done a good job. It was well phrased; with a few exceptions the facts were correct, the arguments were cogent, and the rhetoric was very persuasive. It was likely to convince a lot of people. And it was entirely given over to refuting, point by point, Sam's case for raising taxes.

For example, it agreed that East Salem teachers' salaries were less than those in the surrounding districts. However, it also pointed out that the length of their school day was briefer, their school year 5 days shorter, and several of their fringe benefits considerably more generous. When these things were factored in, the pamphlet argued, East Salem's pedagogues were not so badly off.

Moreover, the brochure put considerable stress on the fact that, whatever their salaries relative to colleagues in neighboring districts, compared to the community's residents East Salem's teachers were living high. The average annual income for teachers was almost $26,000, fully $10,000 greater than the average for other residents—and they earned that sum for 10 months' work, not 12. Why, the brochure asked, should teachers live so well at the expense of those who were struggling to stay off welfare? Sam had to admit that regardless of the merits of this comparison, it was likely to have a powerful effect on voters.

The brochure also scoffed at the idea that every student should become computer literate. It pointed out that as computers became common in the workplace, less skill was required by most jobs, not more. It said that by far the most common use of these machines was in supermarkets, where checkout clerks dragged purchases over optical scanners. Today, store clerks didn't even have to know how to operate a cash register, much less program a computer. Computer literacy was just the latest educational fad, and an expensive one to boot. The brochure went on to cite some educational research to the effect that already thousands of computers were gathering dust in school districts around the country. Were East Salem's residents to pay for a similar distinction? Sam wasn't sure, but he suspected that the brochure's writer just might have his or her facts right about all of this.

But Sam was very sure that at least in a few places the facts were wrong. The brochure claimed, for example, that a district administrator had taken a trip (paid for by taxpayers) that had been primarily for pleasure. It also said that one reason that school costs were so high was because the district had allowed teacher–pupil ratios to get much smaller than was standard elsewhere in the state. Finally, it asserted that the school system had lost almost $15,000 in state funds in the previous year because the superintendent had failed to meet a state deadline. Sam knew that he could show that these claims were simply wrong.

Finally, the brochure closed with a ringing call to arms. All taxpayers were invited to attend an open meeting in the high school auditorium to share their concerns, organize to oppose the coming budget vote, and elect a regular slate of officers. (That's real chutzpah, Sam thought; they want to use school facilities to help them oppose good education!)

Whether or not all of the pamphlet's facts were correct, however, Sam knew that printing and mailing it would have a disastrous effect on the upcoming budget vote. It would certainly sway many to vote "no." And given the probable closeness of the vote, it would only have to sway a few. Perhaps worse, publishing it would certainly help make his board member's worst fears come true. The district would have helped establish and legitimize a permanent, organized, and powerful opposition to good education in East Salem. In the future, getting any budget approved, regardless of its merit and austerity, was going to be harder. Sam wasn't at all sure that he had to be a party to that.

Perhaps the best thing to do was to tell Mr. Foster "thanks, but no thanks." The East Salem Taxpayers' Association would have to take care of its own publicity.

Some Questions

1. We have said that in a free society people have a right to express their opinions. Does that entail an obligation on the part of public officials to help them do so? Is Sam Turner obligated to use school funds to help the East Salem Taxpayers' Association?

2. It is often said that the school must remain neutral when political interests are at stake. That is, if it provides one side of an argument, it should also provide the other. Must it also remain neutral when the political interests at stake are educational in nature?

3. Would Dr. Turner be within his rights to demand that the factual errors in the brochure be corrected if he were to consent to publish it? Wouldn't that amount to censorship?

4. Can the right to express an opinion be curtailed when the opinion will harm others? Is that the case here? Suppose for the moment that East Salem will be unable to attract good teachers unless salaries are raised and that as a consequence children will *in fact* be harmed. Is that fact sufficient grounds for refusing to publish the brochure?

5. What would you do if you were Sam? How would you justify your decision? Is your argument a consequentialist or a nonconsequentialist one?

Two Black Swans

Susan Rossmiller had been taken aback by Steve's question. Steve was one of the brightest kids in her ninth-grade health class, and he often asked penetrating questions. But he had outdone himself on this one. She would have to think carefully about her reply.

The class was studying human sexuality. That was often a touchy subject, and it was especially so in Corinth. The people in the community held fairly conservative views about many subjects, and sex was one of them. Indeed, the introduction of the unit into the health curriculum had raised a small furor: Wasn't it a subject better left to parents? Would it encourage teenage experimentation? In the end, however, the board was convinced that the unit was needed. Figuring importantly in the decision was the fact that the board had a great deal of respect for Miss Rossmiller. She was smart, professional, and sensitive to parents' concerns. She could be counted on to handle the material in an appropriate manner.

Anyway, on this particular morning the subject of sexual abuse had come up. Pupil interest was undoubtedly piqued because of a notorious incident that was even then being tried in the local court as well as the local paper. A good citizen of Corinth stood accused of molesting an 11-year-old girl, and the town was in an uproar. That sort of thing had never occurred in Corinth before. Or at least people didn't talk about it, if it had.

Miss Rossmiller had welcomed the introduction of the topic. She viewed it as presenting an opportunity to educate her students about the subject, to warn them, and to encourage them to report any incidents that they might encounter.

The lesson had been proceeding smoothly when Steve asked his first question: "Is it true, Miss Rossmiller, that sexual relations with children are always bad?"

She hadn't hesitated before replying. "Of course it is. Experts who have studied the problem are unanimous that it is, Steve. Such sex is very often accompanied by assault of the most horrific kind. It's only recently that the problem has been recognized for what it is, a particularly offensive form of child abuse. I think . . . "

Steve interrupted. "I'm sorry, you misunderstood my question. I didn't mean abusive sex, where physical harm occurs. Of course children are hurt by that. Adults are, too, for that matter. I meant a gentle, loving sex. Isn't it possible that an adult and a young person could fall in love? I mean physical love. And couldn't they have a sexual relationship without the young person being harmed? I'm not talking about very young children. Baby girls. But what about older kids—say 10 or so. And suppose that the young person is a boy? Would that always be bad?"

The usual studious notetaking in Health 9 came to an abrupt halt. Steve had the undivided attention of the entire class. Some were looking at him in a speculative manner. A couple of the pupils tittered, and one boy asked if Steve had anyone in particular in mind. Indeed, Miss Rossmiller made a mental note to speak privately with him. Perhaps his questions weren't entirely academic in origin. This time she hesitated before responding.

"Well," she said, "perhaps such things might be possible. There might be no actual physical harm as a result. But as I said earlier, physical harm is only a part of the story. The psychological harm that results can be devastating to a young person. It often scars them for life and prevents them from entering into a really loving adult relationship with their husband or wife."

"Yes, I can see how that's possible," said Steve. "But again, that wasn't quite what I asked. I asked whether or not sex with a child is always bad. The reading we did and your discussion convinced me that it is most of the time. But is it always?"

This time Miss Rossmiller hesitated even longer. "Well, I don't know if it's *always* bad. I'm not even sure that you could find out. What would you do? Run a survey of everyone in the world who's ever experienced it? But, as I've said, all the experts agree that it's very harmful, and it's especially harmful to the personal growth and psychological development of children."

"No, of course you couldn't run a survey," Steve responded. "That's silly. You don't have to do that. If you think that something is always true, there's a simpler way to find out if you're wrong. You go out and search for an instance when it *isn't* true. If you find one, just one, then you know you've been wrong. I remember hearing a teacher in science say that once long ago a person had said that 'All swans are white.' Then another person showed that there was such a thing as black swans. They live in Australia, I think. Anyway, the second person showed that the first was wrong, and he did it by finding one black swan."

Miss Rossmiller leapt at the opportunity. She wanted to end this conversation and get back to the lesson at hand. "That's a very good point, Steve. In fact, that's how scientists often approach their work. They set up a statement—they call it a hypothesis—and then they deliberately go out and try to design an experiment that'll show their hypothesis is wrong. If, after repeated tries, they still can't show the hypothesis is wrong, then they conclude that it must be right. But obviously you can't do that with child abu . . . I mean sex with children. Maybe we should get back to the lesson now."

But Steve wasn't ready to do that. "Well, I don't think that's quite right, I mean about the scientists. I think that if they keep trying to falsify—'falsify,' that's the right word, isn't it?—if they keep trying to falsify a hypothesis and they can't, they can only conclude that the hypothesis probably isn't wrong.

They can't conclude that it's right. At least that's what I learned in science. Anyway, that's beside the point. Isn't it true, that if you could find just one case of a child having sex with an adult where no harm resulted, then you could conclude that sex with children isn't always bad?"

By now Miss Rossmiller had the uncomfortable feeling that she was being backed into a corner. Nevertheless, she was a good teacher, and she recognized that it would be undesirable to use her authority to close down the discussion and get back to the lesson she had planned. So with some trepidation she plunged ahead.

"OK, Steve, I'll grant your point. If we could find one such case, then my 'hypothesis' would be shown to be false. But to the best of my knowledge, there are no such cases. So can't we say that I'm probably not wrong? Again, none of the experts in this area have suggested otherwise."

"Well, that sort of depends on what you mean by 'expert,' doesn't it," Steve said. "I remember reading once about some of the Greek philosophers. Aristotle, and those guys. They were pretty smart. I guess you could call them experts. They were also big on morals. They thought everyone should behave according to some very high principles. Some of them were supposed to be really great teachers. Just like you, Miss Rossmiller. Anyway, the point is that a lot of those guys had sex with the young boys who were their students. I don't think they'd have done that if it was always bad for the kids, seeing as how they were such great teachers with such great morals, right?"

"Look, Steve, I don't know much about Greek philosophers, and maybe they did have sex with their students. But that was a long time ago and in a different culture. Maybe the Greeks of those days thought it was okay. But in our culture, today, it's not okay. We think it's harmful."

"But that's my point, Miss Rossmiller. If something is harmful in one culture and not in another, then it's not always harmful. That's one black swan, isn't it?"

"Well, maybe, Steve. But we don't really know what effects those sexual relationships had on those kids. And besides, perhaps the Greeks had a different idea about what counts as harm. They seem to have had peculiar ideas about a lot of things. And now can we get back to . . . "

"That's a good point, Miss Rossmiller. We can't really know if those kids were harmed. It happened so long ago and everything. But I'm not really sure that it's always harmful to children today and by our own standards.

"You know, Miss Rossmiller," Steve went on before she could interrupt, "I've always been impressed by the way you use outside materials, novels and stuff, to help us learn about health. I've often heard you speak of your love of literature. How we can learn more about human nature and human behavior from great writers than we can from psychologists. I remember your talking about how—what's his name, Vonnegut?—could teach us a lot about right and wrong and good and bad. That's right, isn't it? Novelists can teach us about lots of things, even health?"

"Yes, Steve," said Miss Rossmiller, sounding resigned.

"Well, I haven't read any of the really great writers like Vonnegut, Miss Rossmiller, but I did read a novel by a guy named Nabokov. He's supposed to be pretty good, too. The book's called *Lolita*. It was really funny. Anyway, in the book this old guy falls in love with a young girl. Maybe she was 10 or 12. And he has sex with her. Or at least he does when she lets him, which isn't nearly often enough to suit the old codger. And she doesn't suffer any 'psychological damage.' But he sure does. He spends all of his time following her around like a sick puppy. Talk about psychological damage! She turns him into a basket case. So, there's a second black swan, one from our own times. Maybe sex with children isn't always bad—or at least it isn't always bad for the children. But then, maybe Nabokov wasn't as good a writer as Vonnegut.

"So anyway, I was thinking, Miss Rossmiller. If having sex with children isn't always harmful, maybe sometimes it's helpful. Maybe some kids would actually benefit from it. If we could find one case where . . . "

That's when the bell rang and Health 9 came to an end. In the general bedlam that characterized the changing of classes at Corinth High, Miss Rossmiller had time to wonder what her class had learned today. And she realized that she might have time, if she hurried, to get a copy of *Lolita* from the library before her students got them all.

Some Questions

1. Miss Rossmiller should wonder. Suppose that many of her students left the room firmly convinced that, at least sometimes, it's not harmful for children to have sex with adults. Is that a permissible outcome for a sex education class? If not, why not?

2. Consider a stronger supposition. Suppose that some students left having learned that children can sometimes exert a powerful control over adults, and not be harmed in the process, by granting them sexual favors. Is that a permissible outcome? If not, how could Miss Rossmiller have prevented it without trampling on Steve's right to express himself and on the free flow of opinions in the marketplace of ideas?

3. We have mentioned John Stuart Mill. Mill advocated the free and critical exchange of ideas as the best route to the truth regarding any matter, an exchange much like the one between Steve and Miss Rossmiller. But Mill certainly wasn't thinking of high school health classes. Are there any restrictions that you would consider appropriate on the free expression of ideas in a classroom? If so, what are they?

4. A truly free marketplace of ideas would be one in which the participants are all equally equipped to evaluate the evidence. Can there be such a marketplace? In particular, can a classroom be one? Was Miss Rossmiller's such a marketplace? What problems may arise if some participants in the marketplace are better equipped than others?

5. If you were an administrator, and a parent complained to you about Miss Rossmiller's handling of this class, what would you do?

The Last Straw?

Bill Flemming was in the second year of his probationary period, with one more to go before a tenure decision would have to be made. Gail Bestor, the principal of Westfield High School, had been wrestling with the decision of whether to extend his contract for that year. Until a couple of days ago, she had been leaning toward doing so, but had not really made up her mind. Then "Mr. O." had settled the matter this morning.

Bestor had thought long and hard about Flemming's renewal. In some ways he was an entirely competent, even excellent, teacher. He certainly had admirable rapport with some kids. Just the day before she had overheard a group in the cafeteria discussing him, and several had argued that he was the best teacher at WHS. What they seemed to like most was his ability to challenge their ideas, to make them think deeply about important social issues, and to see others' points of view. Those were certainly important attributes in a social studies teacher. In addition, he obviously was willing to spend a great deal of time with students. Evelyn Whiting, this year's valedictorian, had told Mrs. Bestor that "Bill" took hours of his own time to talk with her about the merits of various colleges, to explain the intricacies of scholarship applications, and even to visit her home to convince her parents that she should be permitted to go to Harvard, thousands of miles away, instead of the local community college, which they had originally favored. "Bill's been infinitely more helpful than our guidance counselors," she had said.

The problem was that most students at WHS weren't in the same league as Evelyn. At best, the majority managed to get through the school and graduate; by every objective standard, academic matters were not their forte. And Mr. Flemming seemed to have little time or interest in working with anyone who didn't have an IQ over 120. He was clearly at his best with highly talented pupils—ones who could follow the intricacies of his arguments and who were able "to think deeply about important social issues," a goal he had often stressed in conversations with Mrs. Bestor.

It wasn't that he was intolerant of average or poor students. They just seemed to fall by the wayside. Gail Bestor reflected that if WHS were made up of Evelyn Whitings, she would rehire Flemming without a moment's hesitation. But it wasn't. Besides, Flemming had another annoying proclivity. He was quick to see injustices, even where none were intended or existed. He was a champion of students' rights and had had several altercations with his colleagues and the administration over incidents in which he thought a student was being treated unfairly. That, in itself, was fine as far as Gail Bestor was concerned. As principal, she sought to be fair, and if she had not been, she appreciated being told about it — privately, and in a professional manner. It was Flemming's style, however, to be confrontational. This tendency and this morning's incident put the last straw on Mrs. Bestor's indecision.

The incident had its roots in a situation that had begun months ago when Mrs. Bestor had appointed a committee of students and faculty (including Mr. Flemming) to draw up a new Code of Student Conduct. When the committee had brought a draft of the document to her three weeks ago, she had insisted on several changes, over the strenuous objection of Flemming and the student members. Basically, Gail had wanted more administrative discretion in student discipline cases, without having a judicial-like proceeding over relatively minor infractions. Flemming and the students seemed to want something approaching a trial before the state's supreme court before a decision could be made or a punishment meted out. In the discussion over these issues, Flemming's confrontational approach had come to the fore, and he had led the student members into something very close to a challenge of her authority. He had also been inflammatory: At one point he had referred to "dictatorial administrators," among whom he seemed to include Mrs. Bestor. When the meeting had broken up, the only agreement that had been reached was to meet again. Gail thought it best to overlook this outbreak on Flemming's part as she tried to reach a balanced and fair decision about his reappointment.

The next time Mrs. Bestor heard about "dictatorial administrators" was over the airwaves as she had driven to work this morning. "Mr. O.," a disc jockey who catered to the musical tastes and doings of the local adolescents, broadcast his lengthy and very slanted view of WHS's new Code of Conduct and its principal. The story included a brief interview with Flemming, in which he forcefully presented his opinions on the matter.

When Mrs. Bestor arrived at work, she immediately called in the teacher to find out where the announcer had gotten his story. To Flemming's credit, he freely admitted that while enlisting the support of "Mr. O." had been the students' idea, he had encouraged them. He said he wanted to illustrate for the students how public opinion could be mobilized on one side of a political issue. When the disc jockey had called him later to verify the students' story, Flemming also consented to a taped interview, the juicier excerpts of which "Mr. O." had aired this morning.

And that was the last straw. Mrs. Bestor decided then and there that she could do without the services of Bill Flemming next year.

Some Questions

1. Are there any limits on Bill Flemming's right to free speech regarding issues in the Westfield School District as a consequence of his being a teacher in that system? If so, what are they?
2. Some people would argue that Flemming's right to express himself is limited by the requirement that WHS be operated in an orderly and effective manner and that the notoriety resulting from the disk jockey's broadcast is detrimental to meeting that requirement. Is that so? How is it detrimental?
3. Flemming's comments during the committee's meeting with Mrs. Bestor might be said to constitute unprofessional conduct. Just what, if anything, is *unprofessional* about publicly criticizing another educator and, at least implicitly, impugning his or her motives?
4. Does it make any difference to the morality of Mrs. Bestor's decision not to rehire Flemming that she had serious doubts about his teaching competence prior to the "Mr. O." incident? How?
5. What would your decision have been if you were the principal? How would you justify it? How might others argue against it? Is there a right decision in this case?

CHAPTER 3

Individual Freedom and the Public Interest

A CASE

Sam Endicott choked and very nearly dropped the glass of beer into his lap. The young woman on the stage bore a remarkable resemblance to Susan Loring, the ninth-grade English teacher at Dennison Junior High School. The gut-slamming music and disorienting strobe lights must surely be affecting his senses, he thought. The woman was not exactly dressed in Miss Loring's usual, rather severe, English-teacher tweeds. In fact, she was not exactly dressed — unless wearing only a sequined G-string counted as being dressed.

Endicott stared at the undulating dancer. The resemblance was striking, but it just could not be. Miss Loring was by far the best teacher he had ever had in his years as principal of Dennison. Everyone on the staff respected her. She was idolized by her students, especially the girls, who, Sam reflected, were beginning unconsciously to ape her speech and dress — to the immense improvement of their own. While she was certainly beautiful — the entire class of ninth-grade boys had fallen instantly in love with her — she was also the consummate professional. Indeed, she had skillfully turned their adulation to educationally constructive purposes. Her obvious love of the Romantic English poets had proven infectious, and Endicott had recently heard some of the toughest boys in his school quoting Keats. The idea that she could be the star dancer in a topless bar was ludicrous.

Nevertheless, he did recall Susan's telling him that she was finding it impossible to care for her seriously ill mother on her teacher's salary and that she was moonlighting on weekends to supplement her income. He had responded that as long as her outside work did not interfere with her responsibilities at Dennison, he had no objection. Since then, he had noted no evidence of any diminution of her teaching competence. If anything, she had gotten better. Perhaps because the strain of trying to make ends meet had been alleviated, she was now even more involved in her profession.

It was at this point in his musings that the music ended and the dancer disappeared behind a curtain as the lights went up. Whoever the woman was, Sam had to admit, she was talented. Instead of the mindless bump-and-grind routine one might expect in such places, her dance had evidenced a sensuous beauty, a lithe grace that approached artfulness.

Sam glanced around at the other patrons—all unfamiliar men. He was uncomfortably aware that community opinion would not be terribly supportive if word got around that the school principal had been seen in a topless bar. He was glad that he was in Belleville, a neighboring town to Spencertown, his own school district. Spencertown would be outraged if such a bar opened within its own borders. Even so, Sam was sorry he had stopped for a beer on his way home from a countywide administrators' meeting. While he firmly believed that his own and his staff's personal, out-of-school lives were no concern of others, he also recognized that his position as a public school administrator might lead some to think that he should hold a different view.

Endicott sighed, put down his glass, and was preparing to leave when he felt a hand on his shoulder and an unmistakable voice say, "Hi, Mr. Endicott! How did you like my routine?"

He swung around to stare into the smiling face of Susan Loring, still in her costume. His embarrassment was bone-deep. He was embarrassed for her, for himself for being seen there, and most of all for his wretched eyes that refused to remain fixed on Susan's face.

DISPUTE

A: Teachers are special. Like it or not, they serve as role models for impressionable young people, and so they have a special obligation to be good that even doctors and lawyers don't have.

B: What do you mean, "good"?

A: Why, morally good, of course! If a teacher lied to the principal when he or she visited the class, or if a teacher stole supplies from the class next door, the students might think stealing and lying were okay. Teachers have to set a good example.

B: Would being a prostitute be setting a good example?

A: Of course not!

B: But what if a teacher was an amateur prostitute only on weekends and traveled to the city to ply his or her trade and no one in the school district knew about it? You can't set an example if the students don't know what you are doing.

A: It is just a matter of time. Someone would find out and then the students would know. It just isn't right. Such a teacher should be dismissed.

B: But don't teachers, or anybody else for that matter, have a right to choose the kind of life they want to lead? What they choose to do on their own free time, as long as it doesn't harm anybody, should be their own business, not anybody else's—not the principal's, not the superintendent's, not the school board's, not the parent's.

A: In public schools, the administration and the board have a responsibility to the community and to the students. What teachers do on or off duty is the administration's business if it might have a negative effect on the students.

B: What do you mean, "might have"? Who is to decide that? And what's negative? Years ago such things as teachers' marrying, going to dances, or drinking in public were frowned upon by some communities and were even cause for dismissal. Teachers have lives, too. They can't be put up on pedestals and hermetically sealed off from the adult world they also live in. That wouldn't be fair.

A: But nobody forced them to be teachers, and being a teacher requires being a very special person, because, like it or not, you are a role model for your students.

B: I don't like it! Sure, in the classroom, I would uphold and radiate community standards, but what I do with my own private life would be my own business.

A: No, as a teacher, it is ultimately the public's business. That's just the way it has to be.

CONCEPT: PERSONAL LIBERTY

Is there anything wrong with Miss Loring's working as a topless dancer? Does her doing so somehow make her unfit to teach? How should we think about such an issue?

First, consider some of the potentially relevant features of the case. It appears that Miss Loring's effectiveness in the classroom is not being impaired. Her students like her and learn from her. Moreover, so far as Mr. Endicott can tell, she does not bring her second profession to school. There is nothing in her dealings with her students that is the least suggestive of sexual permissiveness. It is doubtful that she is influencing the values of her students in a manner that any would consider objectionable. Finally, there is nothing illegal about Miss Loring's second profession.

On the other hand, there is no doubt that her second profession would be regarded as immoral by the majority of the citizens of the Spencerville school district. Most would be shocked by her behavior and would be reluctant to have their children taught by her. Don't their views about the moral character of the people who teach their children count for something? Moreover, it seems quite possible that sooner or later the parents and students of Spencerville will find out about how Miss Loring spends her evenings. While she has been discreet enough to find work outside of the district, someone will surely find his way to the bar in Belleville. On this point Mr. Endicott is exhibit A.

What effect would Miss Loring's second profession have on her students once they knew about it? She is, after all, widely respected by them. Wouldn't this make her a poor influence? Also, it seems likely, should the news leak out, that visits to her place of employment would be high on some students' agenda. Of course, minors are not permitted in the place, but Mr. Endicott had few illusions about their ability to triumph over this trivial obstacle. Then what? After today's performance, Mr. Endicott would certainly view Miss Loring in an entirely different perspective. He wondered what her students would be thinking about while she taught. He was sure that it would go beyond Keats. How are these facts relevant?

Perhaps we might start with the case for Miss Loring. We could argue that Miss Loring's life after school is her own private affair. She should be responsible to the school only for the proper performance of her job. What she does on her own time is none of the school's business. She is accountable to the school only for how well she teaches English to her students. Otherwise the school should have no interest in how she lives her private life.

One of the key features of this argument is the distinction between the *private* and the *public* sides of Miss Loring's life. Perhaps a moral principle of the following sort is being appealed to to justify her privacy. *People can held accountable by others only for those actions that harm others. They cannot be denied the freedom to perform those actions that affect only their own welfare.* John Stuart Mill has put the argument in its classic form:

> . . . the sole end for which mankind are warranted, individually or collective-
> ly, in interfering with the liberty of action of any of their members is self-
> protection. That the only purpose for which power can be rightfully exer-
> cised over any member of a civilized community, against his will, is to prevent
> harm to others. His own good, either physical or moral, is not a sufficient
> warrant. . . . The only part of the conduct of anyone for which he is
> amenable to society is that which concerns others. In the part which merely
> concerns himself, his independence is, of right, absolute. (Mill, 1859/1956,
> p. 14)

We might, then, define private behavior as behavior that affects the welfare only of those who engage in it. Public behavior, by contrast, affects the welfare of others. Democratic governments may take an interest in public behavior defined this way, but a person's private behavior and private welfare are his or her own business.

It might, then, be argued that the reason Miss Loring's second profession should not be the business of her first employer is that it is a private matter. The point is not, of course, that she does it in private. Obviously the point of her job is to be visible. Rather, the idea is that she and her audience are performing actions of their free choice and not interfering with each other. No one is forced to watch. Everyone is there voluntarily. Since everyone involved is a willing participant, there are no grounds to interfere with her behavior. It is a private matter and not the business of her first employer, the school.

These remarks assume a certain way of interpreting Mill's views. If Miss Loring's dancing is to be considered a private matter, it is not because it has no public effects. Obviously it does. It may even have harmful effects. Many would regard her act as morally corrupting. That is presumably harmful. But even so, such harm as may result from Miss Loring's act can be done to others only with their uncoerced consent. If this is the case, then it is they who are responsible, not Miss Loring. So long as all of the participants in any activity are engaged in it voluntarily, it should be considered a private matter. It is only when it affects others in ways they are powerless to avoid that actions become matters of public concern.

A second assumption of the argument sketched above is that the role of a teacher is to be construed narrowly, that is, strictly as job performance. Miss Loring is to be held responsible only for how well she teaches English and not for the influence she might have on her students as a person. It is not especially relevant that she dances on her own time and out of the district. The crucial question is the effect of dancing on her performance as a teacher. If it kept her from preparing her lessons, or if it kept her from getting enough sleep to perform properly in class, the fact that she did it on her own time and away from school would be irrelevant. Mr. Endicott would have a quite legitimate interest if her out-of-school work affected her performance in school. The key question, however, is whether being a good influence on her students is part of her job.

We have not expressed a view as to whether or not topless dancing should be considered immoral. We have only suggested that it is generally believed to be immoral by the citizens of the Spencerville school district. We did this for two reasons. First, we want you to face squarely the issue of whether teachers are responsible to schools for their out-of-school ethical conduct. If you do not view topless dancing as morally questionable, we suggest you substitute something that ethically bothers you. Suppose, perhaps, that Miss Loring had turned out to be a member of the Ku Klux Klan, though that membership had no obvious effect on her teaching. Is being a Klan member all right?

Second, it may be that the key issue is not whether Miss Loring's behavior is immoral, but whether it is immoral according to the moral standards of the community. It is important here to remember that parents are compelled to send their children to school. Yet parents have a legitimate concern for the moral education of their children. To what extent, then, is it permissible for schools to compel parents to submit their children to the influence of teachers whose lives and character the parents find abhorrent?

In retrospect, we have identified two pivotal questions. The first is whether Miss Loring's job as a topless dancer is to be considered as a public or a private action. The second concerns the scope of her job as a teacher. Note that they are connected. If the scope of a teacher's job goes beyond the role of instructor and includes being a good influence on students, that is a reason to hold that any behavior on the part of a teacher that has an adverse effect on the values of students is not a private matter.

This quickly leads to the conclusion that Miss Loring's second job is a matter of legitimate concern for Mr. Endicott. If it is reasonable to believe that her dancing will affect student attitudes toward public nudity or sexual conduct, then her behavior is part of the business of the school system.

At the same time, this argument should be seen as problematic. If teachers are required to be good influences on their students, almost any conduct might be considered to be job related if students knew about it. This would include not only the teacher's sexual life, but matters such as religion or politics. Are teachers to be required to support the dominant religion or political party of their districts? An argument that has this potential consequence surely must be defective.

We believe that its defect stems from the way in which the distinction between public and private action was drawn. Whether an action is part of the public or the private sphere was defined by the scope of its consequences. If an action turned out to have some effect on the welfare of someone else, that led us to treat it as a public act.

However, there are areas of a person's life that should be held to be private even if they have an effect on the interests or welfare of others. Two such areas are religious and political beliefs. These are not considered to be private matters because they have no effect on others. It is perfectly reasonable to believe that a person's religion or politics can influence his or her behavior, which, in turn, has an effect on the welfare of others. Think of the beliefs and actions of the president of the United States, for example. Here there is a different basis for the defense of religious and political beliefs as private.

Religion and politics should be considered private matters because there are compelling reasons why we should respect the free choices of people about them. Religious convictions are often central to people's conception of who they are and what their fundamental duties and obligations are. To treat religious convictions as objects of potential public interest is to open a path for doing great violence to individuals. We treat religious belief and practice as largely a private matter not so much because these things have no public consequences, but because they have such profound personal consequences.

Much the same can be said for politics. The right to participate in the civic affairs of a democratic society is one of the most important of our liberties. The right of individuals to associate with others to advance their political goals is crucial to democracy. A teacher's right to political participation is, therefore, an important right. It should not be subject to control by the school even if it might influence students in a way that community sentiment considered undesirable.

Where does this leave us? We would like to draw two conclusions relevant to thinking about professional ethics. First, it seems reasonable to us to hold that the role of a teacher should be construed broadly enough to include moral education. We would argue that a teacher's influence on the character and moral convictions of his or her students cannot be discounted as unrelated to the teacher's job. Second, however, the area of the teacher's life that should be treated as private and not under the school's control must be determined by balancing the importance of the particular right or interest under consideration against the possible effect of the teacher on students. There are some areas of people's lives, such as religion and politics, where there are strong reasons for respecting privacy unless extremely undesirable consequences are involved.

Other areas are of less importance. If a teacher's preference for garlic for lunch interferes with his afternoon teaching, the school may take a legitimate interest in his diet. It is unlikely that great violence would be done to an individual's freedom of conscience or basic political rights by restricting his garlic consumption. Deciding what is public and what is private is not, therefore, simply a matter of deciding whether an action has an effect on an important interest of the school or of deciding if it might do some harm. It is, instead, a matter of weighing the importance of the kind of privacy involved against the public interest threatened.

ANALYSIS: THE NATURE OF MORAL JUDGMENTS

One set of ideas that is important to the discussion of many moral issues (including this one) is the difference between what we shall call *facts, moral principles*, and *preferences*. Consider an example of a statement exemplifying each:

1. The grass is green.
2. We should always tell the truth.
3. Pickles are better than olives.

The first statement expresses a fact. Factual statements describe. They say something about the world. They are true if the world is the way they say it is. Otherwise they are false.

The second statement expresses a moral principle. It does not claim to describe any state of affairs about the world. Instead, it says something about how the world ought to be. A certain kind of action is obligatory. Moral principles involve concepts such as right and wrong and express duties and obligations. Unlike facts, they are not refuted if they do not describe the real world. "The grass is green" is not true unless the grass is green. But "we should always tell the truth" is not refuted if people lie.

The third statement expresses a preference or a value. Preference or value statements assert that some things are good or that some things are better than others.

These different kinds of statements appear to be true (or false) in different ways. Factual statements are true when they describe the world the way the world is. This does not seem to be true of statements of moral principles or of value statements, however. This is not to say that facts are irrelevant to the validity of moral arguments. If, for example, we believe that it is wrong to cause needless suffering, the *fact* that ridiculing someone causes needless suffering is relevant to establishing the moral judgment that we *ought* not to ridicule that person. This does not, however, turn the moral judgment into a description of the world. Nor is it true because it correctly describes the world. Likewise, statements of moral principles such as "one should always tell the truth" or "slavery is wrong," may contain facts relevant to their justification or "truth," but they are not descriptions; they are prescriptions and proscriptions.

On the other hand, it is not clear that statements of preference are true in any way at all. We know of no way, in general, to decide if pickles are really better than olives. Indeed, we have identified statements of value with preferences partly because we believe that they often are only expressions of individual taste or personal preference and that they do not fulfill general truth conditions. (On the other hand, it does seem possible to have a meaningful discussion about whether Bach is better than rock music.) However, it is our purpose neither to argue about the possible objectivity of some kinds of value judgments nor to deal with the concept of ethical relativity. (We will discuss this issue later.) What is important is to realize that moral judgments and value judgments are different. This is important because the confusion of moral judgments with value judgments is often the source of bad arguments about ethics.

One common mistake is to start from the idea that value judgments have no truth conditions and move, via the confusion of moral judgments with value judgments, to the conclusion that moral judgments have no truth conditions. Statements such as "pickles are better than olives" are treated as though they are identical with statements such as "you should always tell the truth." Both are seen as matters of preference. Neither is true or false. They simply express what we like or how we feel.

This conflation is incorrect. Moral judgments have a different type of content from statements of personal preference. They state that some kinds of behavior are obligatory, not just for oneself but also for others. Moreover, it often seems possible to give reasons for or against them in a way that does not seem possible for statements of preference. If I believe that it is okay to lie whenever I feel like it, it is possible for someone to point out to me reasons why I should not believe this. If I happen to like olives better than pickles, it is not clear how it is possible for anyone to show me that I am in error.

Thus the confusion of moral judgments with preferential value judgments is one reason (a bad reason) for skepticism about the objectivity of moral judgments.

A second problem also results from the confusion between value judgments and moral ones. Generally it is wrong for one person to impose his values on another. If I decide to like pickles or skiing or canoeing, no one has a right to tell me that I must prefer olives or pole vaulting or marathon running. My preferences are a matter of my free choice. But it is a mistake to apply a similar logic with respect to moral principles. On one hand, it is to be desired that people will come to accept their moral obligations freely because they understand that the reasons for them are persuasive. On the other hand, it is often perfectly reasonable to coerce individuals who do not freely accept their moral obligations. The fact that a particular individual is not persuaded of an obligation to abstain from theft or murder is not a reason for permitting him to engage in such behavior. Moral principles express obligations to other people. It is often reasonable to enforce them. The injunction not to impose one's values on others is misplaced if it means that we can never enforce moral obligations.

These observations give us another approach to thinking about the distinction between public and private matters and the scope of individual liberty. We might conclude, given the above argument, that values are private matters, but moral principles are not. Values express our choices as to our own good. We have a right to choose our own values and to pursue them. No one has a right to impose their values on us. Moral principles are, however, a matter of public concern. While it is desirable that people come to their moral principles voluntarily, moral principles express duties and obligations to other people. They may, therefore, be enforced.

Consider how this might be applied to the case of Miss Loring. It might be argued that Miss Loring's behavior and that of those who come to see her involve no moral issues at all. The matter merely has to do with different preferences or values. Miss Loring may enjoy her second profession just as she does her first. That she enjoys it is a reason why she should be free to choose to engage in it if she so chooses. Others enjoy watching. That, too, is their choice. They are merely expressing their preferences.

Of course some may find Miss Loring's performance objectionable. Terms such as *indecent*, *lewd*, or *offensive* are often used to characterize topless dancing. But are these not also expressions of taste or, more accurately, distaste? It is surely true that many individuals in our society would find Miss Loring's performance distasteful. But that, in itself, is not a reason for attempting to suppress it. For if tastes are different from moral principles and if tastes are private matters, to find something distasteful is not necessarily to find it immoral.

If we follow the logic of this argument, we will be led to the conclusion that there are no grounds for Mr. Endicott to object to Miss Loring's second profession. Many of the parents of the Spencerville school district may find her performance offensive. But it is simply a confusion to find it immoral. No issue of morality has yet been identified. Moreover, people have the right to choose their own preferences. In our society part of being a free person is having the right to determine one's own conception of one's good. Others have no right to impose their values on us. But for Mr. Endicott to attempt to get Miss Loring to quit her second job, or to threaten her with termination if she is unwilling to do so, would be to do precisely that. It would be to impose the preferences of the citizens of Spencerville on Miss Loring and her audience. If no moral issue is involved, if what is at stake is a mere difference in preferences, it is difficult to see what justification there is for interfering with these choices.

This argument would be decisive were it not for one further consideration. While generally we believe that people do have a right to their own choices about their own good and that it is improper to interfere with such choices, this principle may not apply when the selection of preferences is inconsistent with some moral principle. Consider an example. Some Americans enjoy baseball. Others do not. It would certainly be unreasonable for those who do not like baseball to attempt to prevent baseball lovers from attending games. Not too many years ago, however, many Americans expressed their preference not only for baseball, but for baseball played only by white people. Can we treat this preference as merely a matter of taste and conclude that no moral issue is involved? Could we argue that those who objected to the segregated leagues had no right to do so and merely were attempting to impose their preferences on others?

We doubt that many of our readers will be willing to accept this line of argument. Why not? The reasons seems obvious enough. Some preferences can conflict with moral principles and thereby lead to conduct that is unjust. Thus while it generally may be the case that preferences are private matters, that is not always true. Preferences can be constrained by moral principles.

To complete this discussion, then, we should ask whether the preferences expressed in Miss Loring's case are inconsistent with any moral principles. Many believe that the preferences expressed by those who watch Miss Loring's second profession are inconsistent with the dignity of women. They find that such preferences lead to the treatment of women as objects and enforce attitudes of male exploitation and dominance. Such arguments seem to be plausible and worthy of further attention. If they are found on further examination to be persuasive, Mr. Endicott possibly will have found a reason to interfere with Miss Loring's second profession.

Our discussion to this point, then, suggests that distinguishing between those aspects of life that are to be left to the decision of the individual from those in which interference may be justified is a complex affair requiring the consideration of a variety of factors. To demonstrate some of this complexity, let us look at arguments for individual liberty as they might be put forth by consequentialists (appealing primarily to the principle of benefit maximization) and nonconsequentialists (appealing to respect for persons).

One type of consequentialism is utilitarianism. It holds that happiness is the ultimate good and that the best acts are those which produce the greatest good for the greatest number. How might a utilitarian reason about individual liberty? Obviously what is required is an argument that shows that not interfering with people in the private sphere of their lives produces better consequences (more happiness) for more people than does interfering. Why believe this? One argument is that individuals are their own best judges of what makes them happy. If I attempt to make decisions about your happiness, I am likely to choose for you that which I value. I may be mistaken about your wants and needs. You are in a better position than anyone else to know what you like. A second argument holds that it is the freedom to decide itself that makes people happy. Freedom is a part of happiness. Therefore, give more people freedom and more people will be happy. A third argument is that freedom provides for experimentation in diverse ways of living, a kind of grand experiment in diverse lifestyles that permits human beings to discover new and valuable ways of living, thereby increasing their own happiness. It also permits society to grow. This, too, promotes the general happiness.

Nonconsequentialists, on the other hand, will appeal to the central notion of respect for persons as moral agents and the conditions necessary for moral agency. Consider three such arguments:

First, respect for moral agency requires respect for free choice. If I am to regard you as a moral agent capable of free choice, I must respect your choice simply because it is your free choice. That you have freely chosen some good as your own requires me and other moral agents to honor that choice. That is a part of what it means to respect moral agency.

Second, granting people freedom to make their own choices is a necessary condition of moral responsibility. We cannot hold people responsible for their choices while, at the same time, interfering with their right to choose. To view people as responsible for themselves is to grant them the right to decide for themselves.

Third, if we object to or interfere with others' choice of their good to further our own interests, we treat them as though they were obstacles to our ends without considering their rights to determine their own ends. If we are to regard other people as moral agents like ourselves, we must show their choices the same degree of respect that we expect them to show ours. To fail to do so is to treat them as means to our ends.

None of these arguments for personal liberty lead to the conclusion that people should be free to do whatever they want simply because they have chosen to do so. All of them require that we find a reasonable way to distinguish between the private sphere and the public sphere. As we have seen, however, this is not an easy distinction to draw. And while we have considered many plausible arguments, we have not solved Mr. Endicott's problem. Nonetheless, we may have learned something about ethics and moral reasoning in the process. Let us consider that possibility.

We began the section on analysis in this chapter by distinguishing between facts, preferences, and moral principles. One reason for doing so was the belief that people are often misled into a position of moral skepticism by bad arguments that seem to turn on labeling preferences and moral principles as values. It is then held that values are matters of taste and that we have a right to our own free choices concerning them. People who claim that it is possible to reason about moral principles are then accused of the dual crimes of seeking to reason about a matter that is merely a matter of taste and of seeking to impose their values on others.

Both of these claims are weakened by distinguishing between preferences and moral principles. The case for treating preferences as matters of taste seems intuitively more plausible than the case for treating moral principles as matters of taste. It is difficult to know how to argue that pickles are better than olives. Even if we can argue that some preferences are better than others, for example, that Bach is better than rock, it does not follow that we can impose our views on others. On the other hand, it is not so hard to argue that murder and racism are wrong or that honesty and keeping one's promises are obligatory.

Also, it makes more sense to apply the principle of noninterference to preferences than to moral principles. We have provided a variety of arguments to show that (other things being equal) people have a right to freely choose their own conception of their good. However, moral principles as expressions of the good are obligatory, and we can interfere with those who breach them. It is the point of moral principles to regulate the interactions among human beings.

These arguments seek to dispose of a common confusion about values and moral principles. They do not, however, show that objective moral reasoning is possible. Indeed, the distinction between facts and moral principles has often been used in an argument to show that moral reasoning cannot be objective.

The essential claim is that moral principles cannot be derived simply from facts. The Scottish philosopher David Hume (1888/1967, pp. 469–470) provided one such argument. Hume noted that one of the properties of a valid argument is that all of the terms that occur in its conclusions are also contained in its premises. Consider:

All men are mortal.
Socrates is a man.
Therefore, Socrates is mortal.

If the argument was slightly changed, we would see a conclusion that did not follow from the premises in the argument (even though it might be true). Consider:

All men are mortal.
Socrates is mortal.
Therefore, Socrates' dog is mortal.

We cannot reach a valid conclusion about Socrates' dog unless the dog is referred to in the premises of the argument. Valid arguments, after all, tell us what follows from our premises. Noting this, Hume then pointed out that it is impossible for any argument containing only factual premises to lead validly to a conclusion about what we ought to do. For any such argument has a new idea in the conclusion that was not in the premises—the idea of obligation. "Ought" conclusions cannot follow from "is" premises.

Do we have a response to this argument? First, it is important to be clear about what follows from Hume's argument. It does not show that moral knowledge or moral argumentation is impossible. If it is correct, it shows only that moral claims cannot be derived solely from facts. Second, syllogistic argument may not be the form moral reasoning takes. We want again to commend our strategy concerning how to develop a view about moral reasoning by engaging in moral arguments and seeing how we construct them.

CONCLUSION

We began with a problematic case. In order to deal with it, we decided that we needed to distinguish between public and private actions. We borrowed one from John Stuart Mill: People are entitled to complete freedom in the private sphere, but they might be accountable to others in the public sphere. Mill's way of making the distinction was tested in two ways. First, we tested it by applying it to other cases. We found some instances where its application seemed to produce objectionable consequences. That seemed to be a reason for modifying it. Second, we attempted to illuminate the concept of individual liberty by seeing how it might be argued for in terms of two abstract moral views that we had sketched earlier, the principle of benefit maximization and the principle of equal respect for persons.

Has this process of moral reasoning that we have engaged in been helpful? It is fair to say that it has not been entirely successful. We and Mr. Endicott still seem to be unsure about what to do in Miss Loring's case. Moreover, we have linked the still-unclear distinction between public and private actions and the complex idea of individual liberty to two different general moral theories, consequentialism and nonconsequentialism, which have quite different views about what is fundamentally at stake. In short, we have made the issue more complicated without resolving it.

On the other hand, we believe that we have made two kinds of progress in our quest to understand the process of ethical reasoning. First, we have learned to use our own moral experiences as evidence for the adequacy of our formulations of moral principles. For example, we rejected some formulations of the public/private distinction because they led to morally counterintuitive conclusions when applied to some cases. We thus offer as one noteworthy feature of moral reasoning the claim that our moral experience, our sense of what is right and wrong in a given case, counts initially as evidence for our moral theories. This is a theme we shall develop later.

Second, even if we have not resolved many of the issues we have raised, we have come to understand what is at stake in them in a more fundamental way. That, in itself, may lead to more responsible moral decisions. But it is also an optimistic sign about moral reasoning. Ethics, like other kinds of thinking, can be a difficult and complex process. That it does not always lead immediately to clear and obvious decisions is not a sign that ethical reflection is impossible. Indeed, that we can come to understand the issues better is a sign that ethical thinking can produce some results.

ADDITIONAL CASES

Tiger! Tiger! Burning Bright

Sharon Athis was obviously troubled. She had come into Smith's office shortly after the semester began and requested an appointment with a counselor. As head of the counseling service at Entwood Community College, Smith was responsible for conducting entrance interviews with new clients. The purpose of these interviews was to ascertain the nature of students' problems and to assign them to the appropriate counselor, if that was warranted. In Sharon Athis's case, it surely was.

Sharon was a somewhat overweight and plain young woman, shy, afflicted with a rather severe case of acne, and very anxiety ridden. In their 30-minute interview she became increasingly distraught. At first she discussed only her weight and skin problems, and Smith suggested that she see a physician at the Entwood Health Service. Sharon greeted this suggestion with silence. When she began to speak again, it became clear that these problems were not what was troubling her. As nearly as Smith could determine, her anxiety had to do with her boyfriend, someone named Blake. However, she obviously could not bring herself to discuss it with Smith. The psychologist guessed that it was a difficulty he often saw in freshman women — a developing sexual relationship that provoked rather severe, but temporary, anxiety symptoms. He suggested that Sharon make an appointment with Dr. Cleis, one of his staff psychologists.

Bernice Cleis was an extremely competent and professionally self-assured person. While she had been on Smith's staff for only three years, having come to Entwood immediately after earning a Ph.D. in counseling psychology, she had quickly established herself as one of the more accomplished members of his team. She was particularly successful with anxiety cases of the sort that Sharon Athis seemed to represent. After Athis left, Smith pressed the switch on his intercom and spoke to Cleis. He described his initial interview and said that Athis would be calling for an appointment.

Several months passed, and Smith thought little more of Sharon Athis. Her case had come up once in a staff meeting, when Dr. Cleis had discussed several therapeutic techniques she had been using successfully with cases of sexual anxiety. In reviewing his staff's appointment schedules, Smith did notice that Dr. Cleis was seeing Athis more often than was usual. He supposed that Sharon's problem was more severe than he had originally thought.

In the spring two events occurred that, taken jointly, worried Smith considerably. First, late one evening after emerging from a movie in a neighboring town, he had seen Dr. Cleis and Miss Athis together. They were laughing and obviously engrossed with each other as they walked arm in arm down the darkened street. Neither saw him. Smith was generally of the opinion that personal relationships between a psychologist and patient were unwise. He made a mental note to discuss the matter with Cleis at an early opportunity.

Even more distressing was a note he received from Dean Lamb the following week. Attached to the note was a letter to the dean from Mr. Athis, Sharon's father, asking Lamb to speak with his daughter. Mr. Athis was very worried. He said that Sharon had become extremely morose and given to crying much of the time while she was at home for visits. Last weekend she had spent the entire time in her room, barely speaking to either of her parents.

Further, Mr. Athis had found a disturbing poem on Sharon's dresser not written in her hand and signed "B," which he enclosed. It read:

> Abstinence sows sand all over
> The ruddy limbs and flaming hair,
> But Desire Gratified
> Plants fruits of life and beauty there.
>   B.

Though Mr. Athis was upset, he seemed to be a reasonable man. His letter went on to say that he realized his daughter was no longer a child and that she was likely to have become romantically involved with some young man. However, Sharon's romance with "B" did not seem to him to be usual. "B" was clearly causing his daughter immense anguish. He and Mrs. Athis were seriously worried about her mental health. He also said that Sharon absolutely refused to discuss her boyfriend with either him or his wife. He closed his letter by apologizing for making an unusual request. He was frightened for his daughter, and he asked that Dean Lamb please talk with her and, if possible, do what he could to help her through a sadly atypical first love affair.

Lamb's note accompanying this letter asked Smith to please call Sharon in and to do what he could for her.

Smith wondered if either the dean or Mr. Athis suspected just how atypical this first love affair might be. While the author of the poem was certainly a male, he was less sure of its plagiarist.

That night Smith stayed late in his office clearing up the day's paperwork. About 9 P.M., in what he thought was an empty building, he was startled to hear a door close and the sound of a woman sobbing. After a moment he realized that his intercom was on and that he was hearing someone in another office. He was reaching over to turn off the device, when he clearly heard Bernice Cleis say, "Sharon, I told you not to go home. I knew it wouldn't help, and I've missed you."

Smith hesitated, his finger on the intercom switch.

Some Questions

1. Would Smith be violating Cleis's right to privacy if he left the intercom on? Does a professional psychologist have a right to privacy in his or her relations with a client?

2. If you answered "yes" to the above questions, distinguish privacy from confidentiality and secrecy. Which of these, if any, does Cleis have a right to as a practicing psychologist? Does it make any difference that Cleis is an employee of a school and not in private practice?

3. What obligations, if any, does Smith have to Sharon Athis?
4. Suppose this case had taken place a few months earlier, that is, when Sharon Athis was a senior in high school. Would that change your analysis? Why?
5. If you were the president of Entwood, would you expect Smith to come to you with the story? If he did, what would you do and how would you justify your decision?

Pregnant

It was the end of the school year, and Helen Nelson was, as usual, very busy. Perhaps that was why she had not noticed Rebecca's pregnancy. Rebecca had called in sick several times during the last couple of months, but Helen really had not thought much about it. Now she would have to think very hard about it.

Helen was the principal of Southwest High School, a large center-city institution in one of the more economically depressed areas of Worcester, a city that was itself economically depressed. The school had a reputation for being "tough," and Helen had to struggle each year to recruit new teachers. Given a choice, most novices headed for the more affluent suburbs that surrounded Worcester, where teaching was supposedly easier. Further, many of the more experienced members of her own staff transferred to other, better, schools within the district if an opportunity arose. Helen had been working on this problem for a couple of years, but so far she had met with little success. In any case, every spring Helen spent a very large part of her time trying to staff her building for the following September. Since March she had been occupied almost entirely in lining up new faculty to replace the inevitable turnover. Finally, that morning, on the very last day of school, she had filled the single remaining vacancy for the next year. Or so she had thought, until Rebecca walked in.

Rebecca Tomlinson's appointment was at the close of the day. Tomlinson was a valued member of Southwest's math department. Indeed, with seven years' experience, she was very nearly its senior member. She was obviously nervous when she entered the office and sat down. After the usual chitchat about summer plans, Rebecca got to the point. She was expecting a baby in early November. "You probably don't know," she said, "but my husband and I have been trying to have a family for several years. So we're pretty happy."

Helen offered her congratulations, though inwardly her heart sank. Now she was going to have to find a math teacher for September, and that was going to be hard. They were in very short supply, and she wasn't sure she would have any luck getting a reasonably competent person. The really good ones would have already signed contracts.

She also began doing a little math herself. If Rebecca was expecting in early November, presumably she had known for at least a couple of months.

Helen was more than a little exasperated that Rebecca had not told her before today. But the worst was yet to come.

"Anyway," Rebecca continued, "I've decided to work as long as I can, probably till the end of October, assuming the doctor continues to say it's okay. Then I'll take the rest of the year off and be back in the classroom a year from September."

"Do you really think that's wise, Rebecca?" Helen said as calmly as she could. "After all, you'll only get in a couple of months of work next fall, and then have to quit. Wouldn't it be better to just stop now and take it easy until the baby comes? Your job will be waiting for you the following year."

"Ben and I have talked about that possibility, Mrs. Nelson, but frankly, it's out of the question. Ben's been laid off, and we simply need the money, especially with a baby on the way."

Helen leaned forward across her desk. "Look, Rebecca. I don't think you realize what sorts of problems this causes. You know that good math teachers are scarce. I'll be doing well to get a certified person in your classroom by September. If I can't offer a job to anyone until November, I may as well forget about it. At best I'll have to take a substitute who's likely to babysit your class for an entire year. You know what kinds of people I've had to get to sub for you. They couldn't teach geometry or trig. I don't think that last guy we got to cover for you could teach fourth-grade arithmetic! It's not fair to the students to stick a sub in there for almost the entire year. These kids have enough problems as it is. Your first obligation is to your students."

"No, Mrs. Nelson, my first obligation isn't to my students. It's to my family," Rebecca snapped back. "I'm sorry if this creates a problem for you and for the kids. If I had a choice about the timing of my pregnancy, or when I take my leave, I would have arranged it to be less inconvenient. But I don't have any choices. So I'm going to be at my desk and ready to teach in September. You'll just have to do the best you can. Besides, district policy is quite clear about this. I'm entitled to a year's maternity leave, and it can begin whenever I want it to, as long as I'm physically capable of doing my job. And Dr. Fischer said he didn't foresee any problems. He thought I could probably work right into my last month."

I'll bet he didn't foresee any problems, Helen thought. What do physicians know about recruiting math teachers?

Some Questions

1. We have tried to draw a distinction between public and private acts. But what sense does it make to think of a pregnancy as a public or private act? Does the public/private distinction help Helen Nelson think about her problem? How?

2. We have said that "others may not interfere with our preferences unless

those preferences themselves conflict with some moral principle. That we find someone's preferences distasteful (or inconvenient) is not a reason for interfering with them." Is there any moral principle involved in this case such that Helen Nelson could rightly interfere with Rebecca's plans for her maternity leave? If you respond that students' needs for a competent math teacher are justification for interference, just what moral principle is that?

3. If you think that there is a moral principle embedded in students' needs, what about the clause in the teachers' contract regarding maternity leave? Isn't that a moral principle? Surely honoring a contract is one. How should these two be balanced?

4. How can school districts avoid this sort of problem—that is, last minute resignations—besides simply relying on the professional commitment of teachers? Try your hand at drafting a policy for Worcester that will balance the rights of teachers and those of the district.

The Aryan Brotherhood

Sarah Katz disdained *The Publican,* so she had missed the article. But after the third phone call in an hour, she went out to buy a copy of the newspaper. She was not particularly perturbed. Even if her callers had correctly reported the contents of the story, she did not put much stock in the whole business. She knew *The Publican,* and she knew Fred Mueller. The former was a first-rate scandal sheet; the second a first-rate physics teacher. When she returned to her apartment with the paper, she set her answering machine to intercept calls, fixed herself a drink, and settled down to read the article.

In essence her callers seemed to have gotten the story right. Apparently *The Publican* had been doing a weekly series on radical fringe groups of one sort or another located in and around Camden. The star of this week's install-ment was a little beauty calling itself "The Aryan Brotherhood," and Fred Mueller was identified as a member of the group.

According to the reporter (who had posed as a recruit in order to get the story), the Brotherhood was a paramilitary organization whose members spent much of their spare time running about in the woods dressed in camouflage, carrying simulated weapons, and getting ready to defend their homes and families after the imminent collapse of U.S. society. The tenets of the organiza-tion included absolute white supremacy, the intellectual inferiority of everyone else, the existence of a Jewish-communist conspiracy, a denial that the Holo-caust had ever happened, and the belief that every (white) citizen had a God-given right to own a heavy machine gun.

Sarah would have dismissed the article and the Aryan Brotherhood with-out a second thought were it not for the prominent place it gave to Fred Mueller, "a long-time member of the faculty of Camden High School." Accord-ing to *The Publican's* reporter, Fred was a lieutenant in the organization and its designated "intellectual leader." The reporter wondered "how Mr. Mueller managed to teach physics to Camden High's minority and Jewish students, when he holds the racial and ethnic prejudices he does."

If the facts were correct, Sarah would wonder, too. But she knew that he did manage to teach physics to blacks and Jews as well as "Aryans." As principal of Camden, she had had ample opportunity to observe Fred, to read his department chairman's evaluations, and to talk to his students. While Mueller probably wasn't the best teacher in the school, he was certainly better than most. More importantly, as far as she knew there had never been the slightest hint of bigotry in anything he said or did in the classroom. Indeed, only a week ago Susan McIsaac, a black senior, had made it a point to praise Mueller to Sarah for the extra time he had spent with her to help her with a particularly difficult unit in the advanced placement physics course. And Susan was not the first black student to make such remarks to the principal.

Before Sarah retired for the night she made a note to herself to talk to Fred in the morning. She was uneasy about even broaching the subject with him. After all, even if *The Publican's* story was completely accurate, she was not sure that Fred's political beliefs, no matter how bizarre, were any business of hers.

As it happened, she didn't need to make an appointment to see Fred. By the time she had finished a couple of routine chores, the first period had ended and Fred Mueller was in her outer office with a gaggle of noisy students in tow, Susan McIsaac among them.

When Sarah had quieted them down, it became obvious what had happened. Many of the students had read the article and had begun questioning Mueller about it as soon as class began. Fred had refused to talk about the story and instead had tried to teach his planned lesson. When they had persisted, some to the point of shouting, Fred had become angry. "My political beliefs and affiliations are none of your damn business," he had said. It was at that point that the period had ended and the whole irate group had trooped down to Sarah's office.

In the office most of the students merely repeated the newspaper's accusations and demanded that Mueller respond. For his part, Fred took the same tack he had taken in the classroom; he didn't have to explain himself to students. Susan McIsaac, however, put the matter in a different light. "Look, Miss Katz, Mr. Mueller's never said anything in class that's out of line or derogatory. But it isn't true that his political and racial beliefs are only his business. From now on, every time he looks at me, or I have to ask him a question, I'll be worried that he'll be thinking I'm another dumb black. I can't learn from a person who I think doesn't respect me."

After Sarah dismissed the students, she sat down to talk with her physics teacher. "You know that I agree with you," she said, "but Susan has a point, Fred. Perhaps you'd like to tell me about *The Publican* story."

Mueller paused a long time before responding. "No, she doesn't, and no, I wouldn't, Miss Katz. Susan doesn't have a point, she has a problem. And it's her problem, not mine. She's reacting to something she's read in a yellow rag. Last week she told me I was a good teacher. I'm the same person I was last week. I haven't changed. I'm still a good teacher. What's changed is Susan's perception and attitude. That's her problem. Second, I wouldn't like to discuss the story with you either. I may be a physics teacher, but at least I know about the Fifth Amendment and my right to privacy—even if you and these high school seniors seem to be entirely ignorant of them. I've said all I'm going to say about this. My political beliefs and affiliations are my own business, as long as I don't try to foist them on my students. And no one can accuse me of doing that."

Some Questions

1. Suppose you are Sarah Katz. What position would you take regarding Mueller's claims? Why?
2. Suppose that the facts in *The Publican* story are absolutely correct. Consider the following line of argument. If Mueller is a history teacher, believing the Holocaust never happened is demonstrable evidence of incompetence in his field. That isn't true, of course, if he's a physics teacher. In the former case then, wouldn't Katz be justified in trying to get Mueller removed from his job, but not in the latter case? Would Mueller's views be more "dangerous" if he taught history?
3. Still supposing that the facts in the story are correct, does it make any difference to your decision in the role of Sarah Katz that these facts were gathered through a subterfuge and that Mueller didn't wittingly and public-ly announce his Nazi-like beliefs?
4. Compare this case to the case concerning Susan Loring's second profession. Does the school have a duty to promote racial tolerance? Does this distin-guish this case from the one concerning Susan Loring? Does the fact that this case involves the right of freedom of association distinguish them?

CHAPTER 4

Equal Educational Opportunity

A CASE

Mr. Bergen had known the politics of this one would be tough. He was now getting an education in how tough. The newly organized Citizens for Excellence was on his case. This was not the year to be against excellence in the Applegate School District. He needed to explain to the board why his decision against putting more money into a program for the gifted and talented was not being against excellence.

Mr. Bergen's district had a unique population mix. For years it had been a farming community. That was still substantially the case. But for the last few years, the district had undergone considerable gentrification. Affluent people from the nearby metropolis had discovered the charm of the rolling hills and pleasant countryside of Applegate. Many of the farmers had succumbed to the lure of the real estate developer's dollars and sold their dairy farms and orchards to the newcomers.

The third portion of the population consisted of migrant workers, most of whom were Spanish speaking. While this portion of the population was fairly small and was dwindling as the farms in the area declined, still about 7% of the children in the Applegate schools were Spanish speaking.

They were a difficult population to work with. The most obvious problem was their poor command of English. Moreover, he suspected that many of the families were illegal aliens. At least they were quite shy of public officials, including him. These problems were compounded by the fact that they were a transitory population. Families would arrive for the fall picking in the orchards. The majority, for whom the working season was over after the fruit was picked, would crowd into trailers to await spring. Their children would start school late and leave early. They might be gone for weeks if their parents found work out of the district. Few of the children would return to the Applegate schools the following year.

Mr. Bergen felt a compelling obligation to help these children. While they were in his district, he felt it his duty to see to it that they got the best education that he knew how to contrive for them. He had badgered the board into hiring a consultant to develop a program. The consultant had produced one that Mr. Bergen thought was first rate. It offered some hope to these children. It was expensive.

Mr. Bergen nevertheless believed that he had a reasonable chance at selling the program to the board. One of the nice things about the newer residents of his districts was that they built expensive homes and had few children. Applegate's coffers had the wherewithal for a new program.

Unhappily, Citizens for Excellence had come up with their own version of a new program. It was an extensive set of new offerings for the district's gifted and talented children. All of the district's new landed gentry seemed to come equipped with at least one child who was thought to be gifted and talented. Some of them really were. This program, too, was expensive. It was clear that there would be only one new program. The only question was which one.

Mr. Bergen favored the program for the Hispanic children. Gifted and talented children had a way of taking care of themselves in this world, especially when their parents were wealthy. The Hispanic children, on the other hand, were in desperate need of a decent education. This seemed decisive to him.

It did not seem decisive to the members of the Citizens for Excellence. They were full of talk about our society's desperate need for mathematicians and scientists, and about how the schools had failed to develop the technological leadership for the next generation. It was of utmost importance to them that we keep ahead of the Russians and the Japanese. Failing to accept their program was positively un-American.

Mr. Bergen was not against scientists, although he was less sure that his primary duty as an educator was to win some contest with the Russians or the Japanese. But he also knew where the power in his district resided. The new residents paid the majority of the taxes. They and the farmers were a substantial majority of the voters of the district. Neither group was overconcerned with the welfare of the Hispanic population. The newer residents thought the Hispanics' crowded trailers and noisy children degraded the neighborhood. The farmers did not believe that people needed to know much to pick fruit. The migrants did not vote.

As Mr. Bergen entered the board building, he knew that if the program for the Hispanic children was to get off the ground he would have to be persuasive tonight.

DISPUTE

A: In this country, we believe in the importance of equality and especially equality of opportunity. Our schools are one of society's most important institutions for teaching the young about equality and for actually providing it. Thus we have special programs for the disadvantaged, those who need a leg up.

B: I agree about equality being a good thing, but something sounds funny here. Doesn't equality mean equal treatment? If you give more resources to one group of students, aren't you treating others unequally?

A: Yes, in a way, but what you are ultimately doing is ensuring that those who were unequal to begin with will have a chance to be more equal educationally with those who are lucky enough to get a good start in life. Equality of opportunity means giving everyone a real chance to succeed and not just giving them equal resources. Besides, these are society's resources, and investing them in the disadvantaged will bring about such social benefits as less crime and more productive workers.

B: Yes, they are society's resources, and just think how much more social benefit might come from investing our resources in the best and the brightest, in our future scientists, doctors, researchers, and inventors! If you are going to provide opportunity, then these are the most important opportunities to provide. To be fair about it, all you have to do is give each person an equal chance to display his or her talent. Then nurture it wherever you find it, even if that means putting more money into programs for the talented few.

A: But that would be giving even more advantage to the already advantaged. Equality and fairness demand that we treat people *differently*. . . . Did I say that? I think I am getting confused.

B: If you think you are confused, what about the students in our schools? We teach them about the importance of equality as a basic value in our democracy, and then proceed to treat them unequally by giving some groupings of students more of our finite resources than others!

CONCEPT: EQUALITY

Mr. Bergen has a problem about equal opportunity. He believes that fairness requires him to provide additional resources for a program for the disadvantaged students in his district rather than for the district's gifted and talented students. Does fairness actually demand this? If the school board votes the money for a gifted and talented program, will that be unjust?

Consider how each side in the dispute might argue for their view. Mr. Bergen seems to believe that the main reason the Hispanic children in his district should have the additional resources is that they need them more. He has appealed to the criterion of need in justifying his choice. Those who have supported the program for the gifted and talented have implicitly argued that the children in this program should receive the additional resources because they can put them to the best use. It is they who will make the larger contributions to the national welfare. Here the assumption seems to be that the criterion for dispensing educational resources should be ability. We should expend disproportionate resources on those who are the most academically able, because it is they who will do the most with them to the benefit of all.

To begin thinking about this choice, consider an additional principle. We will call it the *principle of equal treatment*. It says: *In any given circumstances, people who are the same in those respects relevant to how they are treated in those circumstances should receive the same treatment*. A corollary of this principle is that people who are relevantly different should be treated differently.

What does this principle mean? Suppose we are deciding about admitting two students, Smith and Jones, to a select university. Smith and Jones have received the same score on the admissions test. Should we admit or reject Smith and/or Jones? The principle of equal treatment does not say. All that it says is that whatever treatment we accord to Smith, we must also give to Jones, because Smith and Jones are the same in the relevant respects. The principle also requires that we should have reasons for how we treat people (Peters, 1970). If, for example, we were to argue that Smith should be admitted to the university, we might do so by giving as our reason that the score that he achieved on the test indicated that he had the ability to do the work. This argument logically connects a characteristic of Smith, his test score, to a treatment, university admission. The crucial thing is that any argument that succeeds for Smith must also succeed for Jones insofar as Smith and Jones are the same on the relevant criterion. We cannot, therefore, reasonably argue that we ought to admit Smith but not Jones.

How do we get from the principle of equal treatment to the idea of equal educational opportunity? Often the most important issues regarding equal opportunity concern what we will treat as irrelevant criteria for purposes of access to educational programs. There is a strong presumption that such characteristics as race, sex, religion, and ethnicity are irrelevant to most legitimate educational purposes. Thus if we find that someone is providing different treatment to two individuals in ways having to do with these characteristics, that is compelling evidence that an injustice is taking place. It is not altogether decisive, however. Presumably it is permissible to use race as a criterion in identifying those who are to benefit from a program designed to remedy racial discrimination. And it is legitimate to use religion as a criterion for admission to a theological seminary. Nevertheless, given that race, sex, religion, and ethnicity are irrelevant to almost all legitimate educational purposes, a strong presumption exists that their use as a criterion for the allocation of educational resources is illegitimate.

This analysis suggests that any argument about equality of opportunity will involve three sorts of claims.

1. Moral claims that equality consists in treating equals equally and unequals unequally.
2. Relevancy claims that certain factors are relevant to how people are to
   be treated and others are irrelevant.
3. Efficacy claims that particular kinds of treatments produce desirable
   results.

A full consideration of equality of educational opportunity, then, requires
that we specify the full range of educationally relevant factors and the treatments that are appropriate. It is this that Mr. Bergen is not yet able to do. He
has two groups of individuals who are very different. Presumably both ability
and need are educationally relevant factors. But Mr. Bergen needs to know
how they connect to different kinds of treatments. He needs to know what
counts as fair treatment in this case.

We might approach his dilemma by asking how we can think about it
from both the perspective of the principle of benefit maximization and from
the perspective of the principle of equal respect.

The principle of benefit maximization requires that we look at the problem in terms of the maximization of some good. Let us assume that what we
wish to maximize is a rather vague commodity that we shall simply call
"human welfare." We might also assume that, while human welfare is not
identical with how productive a given society is, a society's productivity is a fair
measure of how well off people are. From the perspective of the principle of
benefit maximization, then, the principle of equal treatment is justified by
arguing that making decisions about people on the basis of relevant rather than
irrelevant criteria is the most efficient use of resources and opportunities. If we
fail to treat equals equally and unequals unequally, we will end up using our
resources and opportunities less effectively than we might and thus not maximize human welfare.

For example, why is it objectionable to take race into account in hiring?
From the perspective of the principle of benefit maximization, the reason is
that it is inefficient. If we consider race in hiring, that means that sometimes we
will not hire the best person for the job because that person is a member of a
certain race. Thus we will get a less efficient worker for our money because we
have used an irrelevant characteristic in deciding whom to hire. The same
argument can be made for educational opportunities. If we are to put our
educational resources to the most effective use, then we will not use such
characteristics as race in deciding who is to receive what opportunity.

We can also appeal to the principle of benefit maximization in deciding
what is to count as a relevant criterion. If we want to know what characteristics
we should look for in a good employee, the answer is that we want those
characteristics that will make that person the most productive. If we are

looking for basketball players, height will be a relevant criterion. If we are looking for accountants, mathematical ability counts. Likewise, if we wish to know about the characteristics that we should look for in allocating educational resources, the question is what characteristics permit people to make the most efficient use of resources.

This argument appears to be the one appealed to by those who are arguing for the program for the gifted and talented. In effect, they have claimed that the reason the district should put its money into a program for the gifted and talented is that that is the most efficient use of the resource. These children are the society's future leaders and scientists. If we spend the money on them, we will be putting our money to its most productive use.

Can Mr. Bergen appeal to the principle of benefit maximization on behalf of the disadvantaged Hispanic students, or can it only be used to justify the spending of our educational resources on those who are the most academically talented? Think about it. It may not be true that spending our educational resources on the most academically able is always the most efficient way to spend them. For example, it is possible that putting extra resources into the education of the most able students will produce little extra benefit. It may be that we would end up spending money to teach these children what they would otherwise learn by themselves. Or it may be that we have reached the point of diminishing returns with these children. Whatever additional learning we purchase for them by creating a new program will be small in relation to the costs involved. Moreover, the benefits for society in a program for the Hispanic children of Mr. Bergen's district may be considerable. These are children who, if their educational needs are not attended to, may be economically marginal for the rest of their lives. If they fail to achieve at least minimal competence while they have a chance to be in school, they may face lives of unemployment. They will become a constant drain on society's resources. But if Mr. Bergen's program succeeds, these same children will have a chance to become useful and productive members of society. Thus it is entirely possible that Mr. Bergen's program for the Hispanic children of his district will have benefits for society that exceed those of the program for the gifted and talented. If Mr. Bergen wishes to persuade his board to invest in a program for the Hispanic children using the principle of benefit maximization, he will have to persuade the board that meeting their needs is the most productive use of the money.

Looking at the idea of equal opportunity from the perspective of the principle of equal respect gives us a different way of seeing the issues, even though there will be many areas of agreement. Those who argue from the perspective of the principle of equal respect for persons, for example, will still wish to distinguish between relevant and irrelevant characteristics. They, too, will insist that treating equals equally and unequals unequally is a moral obligation. Moreover, relevant and irrelevant characteristics will be distinguished in much the same way that they were under the principle of benefit maximization. Relevant characteristics will be those that are relevant to legitimate purposes. In hiring, those purposes will be getting the job done. In education, they will be learning. Nothing about the principle of equal respect for persons requires us to hire people who cannot do the job or to expend educational resources on those who cannot profit from them.

There are, however, some important ways in which the principle of equal respect for persons gives us a different picture of equality. One difference is that equality of opportunity will be argued for in a different way. Consider how we might object to the use of race in hiring from the perspective of the principle of equal respect. Let us suppose that Jones refuses to hire Smith as a carpenter. If Jones's reason is that Smith is not as good a carpenter as some other, Jones has not denied Smith's fundamental worth as a person in refusing to hire him. Jones may continue to regard Smith as a person deserving respect and may consistently continue to think of him as his equal as a human being. He need only believe that there are better carpenters available. But if Jones refuses to hire Smith because of his race, he has rejected Smith's fundamental worth as a human being. When we deny someone an opportunity for some irrelevant reason, we, in effect, say that we are rejecting him because we believe that he is less than a full-fledged human being. We do not want to associate with him for some reason that is fundamental to who he is. Jones could not refuse to hire Smith because of his race and continue to see Smith as a worthy and deserving person, as someone who is his equal as a person and who deserves fair treatment. To deny any benefit or opportunity to a person on the basis of irrelevant characteristics is, therefore, to deny that person's equal worth and to refuse to accord that person equal respect.

A second difference between the principle of equal respect and the principle of benefit maximization is that the principle of equal respect need not require us, in all cases, to select the most efficient use of resources. That use of resources that best expresses equal respect for persons need not be the one that maximizes some outcome.

For example, assume that we know that the program for the Hispanic children would be of some benefit to them. It would allow many of them to achieve some degree of economic stability. But let us also assume (for the sake of the argument) that the overall economic impact of the program for the gifted and talented would be greater. Given these assumptions, the principle of benefit maximization produces an obvious choice. We should choose the program for the gifted and talented. Is that the only defensible choice? Mr. Bergen might respond that it is not. Despite the assumption that the program for the gifted and talented has a larger overall impact, the program for the Hispanic children is more crucial for them as persons. It will make the difference for them between economic marginality and stable and productive lives. Even if the overall impact of the program for the gifted and talented would be greater, the need of the Hispanic children overrules it. It is unfair to deny them this chance for a better life. There are times when meeting the need of some is more important than maximizing the average welfare of all.

Mr. Bergen's claim also might be argued for by appealing to the principle of equal respect. If human beings are of equal value, then their interests and their welfare are of equal value. But the principle of benefit maximization does not always respect each person's interests and welfare equally. Sometimes it seems to tell us that we may trade the welfare of some for the welfare of others. Indeed, we may do this whenever the average welfare increases. But to do this is to treat some people as though they were merely means to the welfare of others. It is to fail to treat their interests and welfare as of equal worth with that of others. It is to fail to respect them as persons.

Thus, the principle of benefit maximization can conflict with the principle of equal respect when it requires that we trade the welfare of some for the welfare of others. There are times when this seems unfair. Can we ever justify unequal treatment? What might be an alternative? Suppose we held that we were only permitted to have an unequal distribution of some resource when those who received the lesser share benefited as a consequence, a perspective given in-depth examination by John Rawls (1971). We will call this the *maximin principle*. It requires us to maximize the welfare of those who receive the minimum share. In the case at hand, this would mean that we should prefer the program for the Hispanic students so long as this program produced greater benefits for them than those that would result for them from spending the money on the gifted and talented. We would do this even if spending the money for the gifted and talented produced higher average benefits.

The maximin principle has three features of note. First, while it does not require that all benefits be distributed equally, it does require that inequalities (departures from an equal distribution) are to be permitted only when everyone benefits as a result. Inequalities may only be justified by showing that those who receive the lesser share are nevertheless better off than they would be under an equal distribution. What is forbidden is inequalities that trade the welfare of some for the welfare of others.

Second, this principle is especially attentive to the needs of society's most disadvantaged. It requires, in effect, that we may only distribute resources in such a way as to result in their benefit. We may not distribute resources so as to promote the average welfare if the disadvantaged are made worse off as a result. The welfare of the least advantaged, not the average welfare, is made the touchstone of social justice.

Third, this principle seems to respect everyone equally. While it does not require that everyone be equally well off, it does prevent some from being well off at the expense of others. Inequality in the distribution of resources is permitted only if all benefit.

Does this help Mr. Bergen? Very likely it does. It gives him a way of thinking about his choices that supports his feeling that justice requires paying special attention to the needs of his district's disadvantaged students.

ANALYSIS: MORAL EXPERIENCE

In the preceding discussion we introduced a new moral principle, the principle of equal treatment. This principle requires us to treat people who are similarly situated in some relevant way the same and people who are differently situated differently. We found that we could argue for this principle by appealing either to the principle of benefit maximization or to the principle of equal respect. Both appeared to require it, but for different reasons. It also turned out, however, when we looked at a specific case concerning the gifted and the disadvantaged and how resources were to be divided between these two quite different groups, that the principle of equal treatment was insufficient to decide the matter. We had to return to the basic principles of benefit maximization and equal respect. However, this produced conflicting results. It appears, then, that we should begin to ask whether there are any reasons why we should prefer one of these basic principles to the other? Let us consider some arguments.

One objection to the principle of benefit maximization is that, on occasion, it appears to justify results that seem intuitively unfair. In our case it seemed as though it might justify denial of an important educational program to children with a desperate need. There is a stronger case than this that can be made against the principle of benefit maximization, however.

It is important to recognize that the principle of benefit maximization will justify *any* exchange between the welfare of one group and the welfare of others so long as the average welfare increases. What the principle demands is that the average welfare be as high as possible. Suppose, then, that at some historical moment slavery was the most productive economic system. Does the principle of benefit maximization justify slavery? It appears that if it is, in fact, true that people are on the average better off in a society where some individuals are owned by others, then the principle of benefit maximization would justify slavery. But surely any moral principle that can justify something as morally offensive as slavery must be suspect.

Moreover, slavery is not the only morally problematic potential consequence of the principle of benefit maximization. It appears that any human right might be threatened if its denial leads to an increase in the average welfare. In chapter 2 we appealed to the principle of benefit maximization to justify intellectual freedom. We argued that individual freedom was efficient in producing the cumulative happiness of all. But suppose there were cases in which the consequences were otherwise. Perhaps there are circumstances where freedom is not conducive to the overall happiness. Ms. Fitzgerald's superintendent, Dr. Higgins, believes this about her case. Does it follow that we must suspend freedom in such cases? It appears that the principle of benefit maximization would require it.

It seems, then, that the principle of benefit maximization is a potential threat to basic rights. Not only does it permit us to trade the welfare of some for the welfare of others, it also allows us to trade the fundamental human rights of some for the welfare of others. All that matters is that the average welfare increase. This counts heavily against the principle. The principle of equal respect, however, has no such consequences. Its central requirement is that we respect the rights of others and not trade rights for welfare.

This suggests that consequentialist theories generally have a kind of liability that nonconsequentialist theories do not. They justify basic human rights only when and if the consequences of these rights are desirable on the average. Otherwise, consequentialist theories can lead to trading the rights of some for the welfare of others. Is this decisive? Before we bury the principle of benefit maximization and consequentialist ethical theories generally, we should attempt some defense of them. Consider two arguments.

First, consequentialists often argue that the imagined undesirable consequences of an application of the principle of benefit maximization are just that, imaginary. Take the case of slavery. If enslaving some people increases the average welfare of a society, then the principle of benefit maximization justifies slavery. But are there any real circumstances in which slavery would make society better off as a result? Consequentialists are likely to argue that when we look at the full range of slavery's consequences in any society, the answer must be "no." Perhaps some economic efficiencies might result from slavery in some cases, but consider other consequences. A slave-holding society must put much of its resources into means of oppression. It must have numerous police, soldiers, and overseers. Besides the fact that these individuals are unproductive, they can become threats to the liberty of the owner as well as the slave. Moreover, slavery has undesirable consequences for people other than the slave. The owner must live in fear of the slave. In these ways, the institution of slavery generally weakens the fabric of society. A slave-holding society must be fractious and unstable. Therefore, no actual slave-holding society can satisfy the principle of benefit maximization. That, after all, is why slavery is unjust. In real cases, consequentialists argue, the principle turns out to lead to an affirmation of human rights, not to their denial.

Second, nonconsequentialist views can also have troublesome results. In the previous section of this chapter, we argued that the maximin principle gave best expression to the principle of equal respect for persons. Inequalities are permissible only if they benefit everyone, especially those who receive the lesser share. But this might, under some circumstances, require us to forgo very substantial gains for almost everyone if only a few were benefited thereby. Suppose that a private school received a very substantial facilities gift, enough to build a needed modern library and to add a gym or swimming pool to their nonexistent physical education facilities. However, their rich benefactor made the gift with the stipulation that it be used in accord with a maximin principle. Therefore, the headmaster decided to spend all of the money to accommodate one paraplegic student with very expensive special equipment and substantial building alterations, including elevators, which, of course, all students could use to their benefit when they were not being used by the most disadvantaged student. Is that fair? Is it not sometimes morally appropriate to trade the welfare of one or the few for the welfare of the many? Are the many to be held hostage to the few? Thus, there is something to be said for consequentialist views and the principle of benefit maximization.

Are these considerations helpful? Obviously, we have not decided the issue. But we have learned something about the structure of the arguments for and against two general views of morality. It appears that when the principle of benefit maximization clashes with the principle of equal respect, the central concern is the extent to which we are willing to allow certain kinds of trades. When, if at all, are we willing to trade the welfare or the rights of some for the welfare of others? Are basic human rights negotiable? Can we suspend them if the general welfare requires it? If we have not resolved the dispute, at least we have achieved greater clarity about its nature. We also have a better idea of what is at stake when we make moral choices, even if it is more complex than we might like it to be.

Have we learned anything about moral reasoning? Here, as in the previous chapters, we have tested the moral principles that seem basic to our moral theories by deriving their consequences and by testing these consequences against our moral sensitivities in specific situations. For example, we generated some doubts about the adequacy of the principle of benefit maximization by noting that under some circumstances it appears to have morally abhorrent consequences. We tested the maximin principle in a similar way. This play between situations, principles, and intuitions is a characteristic feature of moral reasoning.

We appear to be engaging in a general process of encountering a situation in which some moral choice is required and to which we have a certain intuitive moral reaction. Mr. Bergen, for example, felt that it was unfair for the available resources to go for a program for the gifted and talented when there were other students who were far more needy. He was not, however, clearly able to say why. One way to help achieve clarity about our moral intuitions is to attempt to state a moral principle or principles that might serve to justify them. When we are able to formulate a principle that underlies our feelings, we then proceed to test that principle against other cases. We ask what the consequences of applying this principle might be in different situations. If we find that these results are also consistent with our moral experience, then that is a reason for accepting the principle. If, however, the principle seems to have morally objectionable results when applied to other kinds of cases, that counts against it. We thus test our moral theories against our moral feelings, much as we test scientific theories against data.

We also can achieve a higher degree of clarity about what is at stake in our moral choices by developing our moral theories. Linking issues about freedom and equality to principles such as the principle of benefit maximization or the principle of equal respect has helped us to develop our moral theory by appealing to moral ideas that apply to a broad range of cases. We can thus test our moral ideas against a broader and more adequate range of possibilities. Moral reasoning, then, seems in some respects like other forms of reasoning. It is logical and objective, considering all possibilities and legitimate criticisms. It involves both constructing theory and testing the consequences of theories against experience.

CONCLUSION

Note also that while we have not resolved the tension between the two major moral theories with which we have been dealing, we have made some progress. We have shown, for example, that some important ethical ideas have considerable justification. For example, the principle of equal treatment has been tested successfully against our moral experience. Moreover, it seems theoretically consistent with the principles of both benefit maximization and equal respect. That counts strongly in its favor. That we have not solved every problem we have raised should not be too discouraging. We have, after all, tried to raise the difficult problems. And we have at least achieved some clarity about them. That seems reason for optimism about the possibility of objective moral reasoning.

ADDITIONAL CASES

Can Mathematicians Reason?

Gauss Function, the head of the mathematics department at Boston Scholar High School, had agonized over his decision for too long already. He would have to write his letter of recommendation today, if it was to reach the

Integral Institute before the fellowship deadline. He would have to decide among Elizabeth Fitzgerald, Charles Miller, and Ramon Ortega.

Each year 10 Integral Summer Fellowships were awarded to high school juniors who were going on to study mathematics in college. Fellows spent their summer at the Integral Institute in California working with some of the nation's top mathematicians. The competition for these awards was intensely keen. The best students in the entire nation would be competing. Winning an Integral Fellowship virtually guaranteed admission to the best universities in the country.

The primary criterion to be considered, according to the fellowship form, was "creative promise," the candidate's potential to do original mathematical research. Obviously this criterion required a highly subjective judgment from referees. While high school grades and test scores would be considered, the form stressed that they would not be determinative. The application also stressed that the Integral Institute was especially interested in promising minority and women students.

Function knew that his nominee would be accepted. Don Von Neumann, the head of Integral, would place commanding weight on any recommendation he submitted. Function and Von Neumann were old friends. They had earned their Ph.D.'s together at Yale, and they had kept in touch over the years. While Von Neumann had gone on to a distinguished career in mathematical research, Function had dropped out of what he termed "the academic rat-race" to take up high school teaching, because, as he said, he wanted the chance to help develop young minds and introduce them to the beauty of mathematics. Despite his career choice, Function continued to do scholarly work in mathematics and to contribute to research journals. Von Neumann often said that he admired his old friend's ability to teach in a high school and simultaneously be a practicing mathematician.

Whenever Von Neumann came to Boston he always looked up his friend, Gauss Function. On one of these occasions he had talked of the Integral Fellowships. He had said that, in choosing fellows, he rarely looked at grades or test scores. "Mathematical creativity isn't measured by such trivial aspects of academic culture," he had said. "Give me the considered assessments of people whose judgments I can trust."

Function knew that he was one of the people Von Neumann trusted. He also knew that he was in essential agreement with his friend; only creative mathematicians were qualified to recognize creativity in their students. However, Function was also acutely aware that the practical result of this was to create what some people would refer to as an "old-boy network." Hence, Function was always especially attentive to affirmative action considerations. He believed that in the past women and minorities had been unfairly discriminated against in mathematics, and he vowed to do his bit to overcome this legacy whenever the opportunity presented itself. In the present case he wasn't sure if one had.

On the one hand, if GPAs and test scores had been critical, Function's task would be simple: Elizabeth Fitzgerald would win his support hands down. The young woman had a 4.0 GPA and 800s on the SAT. By objective measures she was a gifted student. He was less sure of the originality of her mind, however. He had glimpsed only flashes of the creativity that separates gifted researchers from pedestrian ones. He was sure Fitzgerald would be a competent mathematician; whether she would be an outstanding one was problematic.

On the other hand, Charles Miller seemed to have the greatest potential for creative research. In class the young man was often brilliant and raised startlingly perceptive questions. The problem was that he wasn't always around to ask questions. He skipped many of his classes; he was disdainful of subjects that didn't interest him; he was an unbridled egotist. Partly as a consequence of these qualities, his grades were abominable. Mostly, however, his dismal record was a result of his simple refusal to do work that, he claimed, "bored" him. While Miller said he was going on to do mathematics in college, Function doubted whether any good department would accept him. He certainly wouldn't get in without an Integral Fellowship.

But Miller's personal characteristics made Function wary of recommending him. Function suspected that if Miller found the Integral Institute "boring," he would the summer on a California beach surfing and smoking dope. Frankly, Function didn't like risking his standing as a judge of talent by recommending Miller. If the young man "bombed out," Function suspected that his future nominees to Integral would no longer be assured of acceptance.

On the third hand there was Ramon Ortega. On paper Ortega's record was far superior to Miller's but nowhere near Fitzgerald's. He was a straight A student in math, but only an average one in his other subjects, with good but not outstanding SATs. He rarely spoke in class, and Function had no clear idea of how gifted he was. The department head suspected that much of Ortega's trouble stemmed from a manifestly poor elementary education, but he was unsure of this. Thus, on the major criterion of creativity, Function considered Fitzgerald and Ortega essentially equal (and relatively unknown) quantities. Miller, he was sure, had more potential.

It was when he considered affirmative action criteria that he found himself in a real quandary. Fitzgerald was as close to being a genuine aristocrat as U.S. society could produce. She was the scion of an old Boston Brahmin family. The Fitzgeralds (and their money) had been around almost as long as Boston had. With her academic record and her family's wealth, prestige, and political clout, she was certain to gain admission to any university in the country. She certainly did not need a fellowship. Nevertheless, she was a woman, and women were badly underrepresented in mathematics. A fellowship would certainly give her career a boost. On the fourth hand, then, Function wondered whether Fitzgerald's sex was really relevant to his decision. Could being a female ever be a real handicap to anyone who came from the Boston Fitzgeralds?

But if Fitzgerald's sex was relevant, despite her magnificently endowed background, what about Ortega's ethnicity? Function was as troubled by Ortega's status as a Hispanic as he was by Fitzgerald's sex. It turned out that Ortega had not been born in Puerto Rico, but in Boston, as had his mother (whose maiden name was Smith, Function discovered). Mr. Ortega was from Puerto Rico, but he had been in Boston since early childhood and was now the proprietor of a successful construction firm. While hardly from the same social stratum as the Fitzgeralds, the Ortega family was solidly bourgeois. On the fifth hand then, should Ramon really be considered disadvantaged or Hispanic for affirmative action purposes?

Finally, on the last hand of this n-dimensional space, there was Miller. He was the quintessential WASP. Born and bred in a Boston suburb, the sole son of middle-class professionals, he had nothing to recommend him for affirmative action purposes. Indeed, he represented precisely the sort of person whose ubiquity affirmative action was designed to curtail. Should Miller's WASPness count against him?

Gauss Function considered these things as he sat down to write his old friend Von Neumann.

Some Questions

1. Affirmative action is a national policy designed to right past wrongs done to minorities and women. Does righting those wrongs necessarily require the commission of another wrong against nonminorities and men?
2. How might affirmative action be carried out so as to avoid such wrongs? Be specific. That is, write a policy for the Integral Institute that will increase the representation of women and minority members in mathematics, while avoiding an injustice to other groups.
3. How does your suggested policy for the Integral Institute stack up against the principle of equal treatment we discussed under "Concept: Equality" earlier in this chapter?
4. If your policy violates the principle, can you justify the violation without recourse to an argument resting on righting injustices done in the past to women and minorities?
5. Suppose that our description of Miller's abrasive personality and unwillingness to do "boring" work had been omitted from the case, but all else remained the same. Would your choice of who should receive the fellowship change? If so, why do sex and minority status only count when weighed against personality quirks?

Bigotry?

Normally the meetings of the New Athens Administrative Cabinet were prosaic affairs. Indeed, Sarah Brownell, the superintendent, sometimes had difficulty keeping her principals awake. The details of budgets and personnel policies often had a soporific effect when they followed hard on the heels of a school cafeteria lunch. But today the meeting had grown increasingly tense. The longer Fred Katz spoke, the more restive everyone had become.

Fred was the principal of New Athens High. Its head for over 20 years, he was a quiet, thoughtful man whose forte was the meticulous analysis of problems followed by carefully considered action. Changes were not instituted frequently at NAHS, but when they were, they were usually appropriate ones. He also had a reputation for being plainspoken and not taking kindly to criticisms of his school if he thought they were unjustified.

As Fred spoke, Sarah had noticed that several of her principals were glancing surreptitiously at Jim Crawford, wondering how he was reacting to Katz's statements. Jim was staring very hard at Fred, but he was not saying a word. Finally, the tension had become palpable, and Sarah had interrupted to say something to the effect that nothing could be decided today anyway and that they had to get back to the agenda if they were to finish at a reasonable time. But even after an hour spent on the intricacies of the bus schedules, the air was still charged when everyone left. Everyone except Jim Crawford, that is, who stood waiting in the hallway. "Can I talk with you for a few minutes, Sarah?" he asked.

Jim was New Athens's only black principal. Sarah herself had appointed him to head Jefferson Elementary School shortly after she had become superintendent two years ago. She was committed to school integration, including the integration of the district's professional staff. She thought such an appointment was especially important because the community's black population had grown substantially in recent years. She was pleased with her choice. Jim was a good educator and a dynamic leader; already she was beginning to see the effects of that leadership at Jefferson. Staff morale was high, pupil achievement was increasing, and a number of parents, both white and black, had spoken highly of him. In fact, it was Jim's initiative that had provoked his remarks to Fred Katz during the meeting.

Jefferson Elementary, Jim's school, was a feeder to New Athens High, and he had become interested in the educational careers of Jefferson's graduates when they entered the secondary phase of their educations. In following up on that interest he had interviewed some former pupils, talked to the guidance counselors at NAHS, and collected some statistics. During the "new business" part of the meeting, Jim had presented the results of his work.

He began by describing the tracking system at the high school. Its curricula, like those of many U.S. secondary schools, were divided into college, general, and vocational tracks. Most of the students in the first track went on to the state university. A substantial number of those in the general track either went to the local community college or took white-collar jobs in the numerous electronics firms in the area. But according to Jim's figures, most of the students in the vocational areas took blue-collar jobs, entered military service, or were currently unemployed.

Also like most tracked secondary schools, NAHS's tracks were closely associated with race, Jim said. Fifty percent of the students in the vocational curriculum, 30% of those in the general track, and only 20% of the college-bound group were black.

Jim saw these figures as indications of inequality of opportunity in NAHS. "What's happening over at your shop, Fred?" he asked the high school principal. "Most of those black kids are coming out of my school, and I think they've been adequately prepared. Why are they being shunted into the bottom track?"

The question caught everyone's attention. Fred, as was typical, took the time to scrape the dottle out of his pipe before replying.

"You know, Jim, I wondered about the same thing a few years back, and I took the time to study the matter carefully." (Sarah smiled inwardly. In a single sentence Katz had managed to suggest that he was way ahead of Jim in recognizing a problem and that Jim hadn't given it adequate thought.) "I don't recall the details of my investigation, but the gist of it was as follows:

"I remember being concerned about possible racial bias in my staff. But the fact that a number of black kids were in the college track at least suggested that if the staff were biased, they were being selective about it. They couldn't have been prejudiced against black students per se. Then I interviewed almost half of the kids in the vocational track. It wasn't anything formal, you know, just casual conversations in the halls and so forth. Nearly all of them told me that they were in the vocational track because it's where they wanted to be. They don't want to go to college. They like it. They like taking auto mechanics, cosmetology, or the food service program.

"And those are good programs. Just a week ago, in fact, I was speaking to Ruth Higgins, a woman who runs a beauty shop over on the west side of town. Most of her customers are black, you know. Anyway, she'd just hired one of our girls, and she was telling me how well she's doing. Said the girl had obviously learned a lot in the cosmetology program.

"Now it happens that I know the kid she was talking about. She'd been a hell of a problem for her first couple of years in high school. Mother's the only one at home, a raft of kids, drunk half the time, a series of boyfriends streaming through, welfare—the whole bit. And the daughter looked like she was heading for the same sort of life. Instead, the kid got interested in cosmetology, started getting passing grades for the first time in her life, hung in there, and graduated. If we'd stuck her in the high track studying American literature and algebra, she'd have been in over her head. She'd probably have dropped out and be on welfare today. Instead she's got a job and a decent start in life. What's wrong with that?

"I also talked to some of the parents. Most of them aren't interested in sending their kids to college. Kids aren't just stuck in the vocational programs, you know. We look at their test scores. We consider the recommendations of their elementary teachers. But most of all, we talk to the students and to their parents. They participate in the choice of curriculum, when the decision is made in the ninth grade. We explain the advantages of each of our programs. And then the parents, the students, and the guidance counselors decide together. But the parents and the students always have the final say. We'd never put a kid in any track if they wanted another. If the kid looks like he or she can handle the academics, we encourage them to enter the college program. But many don't want it. What are we supposed to do? Put them in a program against their wishes because it looks better for us to have racially balanced tracks? Or maybe we're supposed to abolish the tracks altogether, so everyone has to study Shakespeare, trigonometry, and French, whether they're able to master those things or not and whether they're going to college or not.

"Finally, don't take what I'm going to say wrong, but let's face facts, even when they're unpleasant ones. Every piece of evidence I've ever seen points to the possibility that black kids, *on average*, aren't as *academically* talented as whites. Maybe it's because of 'socialization,' whatever the hell that means. Maybe it's because their peer culture doesn't value academic success as much. Maybe it's because of the disintegration of the black family. Maybe it's because of America's history of racism. And maybe, just maybe, it's because black people aren't as intelligent as whites. I don't know, you don't know, and neither does anyone else know. Anyone who says they do is either a fool or a liar. If . . ."

It was then that Sarah Brownell interrupted and called the meeting back to its agenda.

When Sarah and Jim entered her office after the meeting, Jim had exploded. "Look, Sarah, Katz has got to go," he began. "I couldn't believe that a man as intelligent as he would mouth the racist crap that he did. The black kids in this town have got to have a chance at a better life. I don't have to recite the statistics on black poverty, unemployment, and youth crime in New Athens. You know them. And schooling is their chance. Maybe their only chance. Funneling them into cosmetology and food service occupations is a bad joke. That's no chance at all.

"When I started looking into this problem, I knew what I'd find at NAHS—that most of the black students were in the lower track. That's true in most schools. What I didn't expect to find was a principal who thought that that's where they belong. 'Maybe it's this. Maybe it's that. And maybe, just maybe, it's because black people aren't very smart.' Jesus! Well, there's another 'maybe' he left out. Maybe it's because our high school principal is a bigot.

"Katz is smart, I give him that. But racism is a disease that infects smart people, too. I'd hoped that when I discussed this problem with Fred he'd put his intelligence to work to help solve it. But he's not part of the solution, he's part of the problem. Nothing will happen at that school while he's the principal.

"Get rid of him. If you have to, 'promote' him to some harmless job in the central office, while you still have the chance. Once this gets out there'll be hell to pay. And it will get out—there were 12 people in that room today besides you and me. The black community in this town won't tolerate those sorts of attitudes anymore."

Sarah told him that she needed some time to think over the whole incident. But she knew she wouldn't have too much time. She recognized the thinly disguised threat in Jim's last remarks.

Some Questions

1. Fred Katz's comments to his colleagues are a mixture of facts and opinions. Which are which?
2. Assume for the purposes of discussion that the facts regarding how NAHS students get placed in tracks are correct—for example, that parents and pupils have the final say, that they are presented with an unbiased description of the advantages and disadvantages of each track, and so forth. In those circumstances, do Katz's opinions make any difference? How?
3. We have said that people have a broad right to express any opinions they wish, without fear of governmental interference or punishment. If Sarah gets rid of Katz, will he have been punished for expressing an unpopular opinion?
4. Are there any special restrictions that should be applied to educators' opinions regarding race that should not be applied to any other citizen? If so, what are they?
5. Suppose it is true that pupils at NAHS are placed in the track that they and their parents want. On what grounds does the school have an obligation to try to convince them that they are wanting the wrong thing? Is racial balance one of those grounds?
6. Does Katz have any right to expect that opinions expressed to colleagues in a private, professional meeting will be treated as confidential communications? If someone "leaks" Katz's comments to the public, would that person have acted unprofessionally?

Little School, Big Problem

In Fred Hastings's professional opinion, the North Creek School District was simply too small. Perhaps the time had come for him to act on that judgment and annex the district to Esterville.

Hastings was the commissioner of education for the state of Columbia. As commissioner, he was responsible to the state board of education for the effective and efficient operation of all of the schools in the state. He considered the North Creek School District to be neither effective nor efficient.

The school system had a total K–12 enrollment of only 254 pupils. Last year its graduating class had consisted of 15 students. Further, its enrollment had been declining for a decade. If present trends continued, it could be below 200 in five years. With those kinds of numbers, it simply could not offer an adequate educational program—at least not without levying astronomical taxes on its residents. And the people of North Creek could barely afford their current modest school taxes, much less astronomical ones.

Esterville, on the other hand, was a moderate-sized town only 15 miles to the west of North Creek. Esterville School District enrolled something over 3,000 students and offered, as nearly as Hastings could tell, an entirely adequate education to its pupils. Further, Esterville's school-aged population had also been in decline, and so it had plenty of room in its elementary and secondary schools to absorb North Creek's students. In fact, the Esterville Board of Education had recently indicated its willingness to annex its Lilliputian neighbor. The road connecting the two districts was a good one, so it would be easy to bus North Creek's pupils into the larger town for their education.

There were a lot of very good reasons to do just that. Because North Creek was so small, it was unable to offer many of the courses that were routinely offered to pupils in other districts in Columbia. For example, French was the only foreign language that the school system offered, and it provided only two years of that. Last year two of its second-year French students had requested another year of that language. Obviously the district couldn't afford to pay a teacher to instruct a class of only two students, and so the students went without. However, Esterville offered four years of French (and four of German). If North Creek were annexed to Esterville, students who wanted advanced levels of a foreign language would be able to take them. The same situation obtained in most of the other academic and vocational subjects—calculus, computer programming, and farm mechanics were just a few of the courses that would be available to North Creek students if they were bused to the neighboring district.

Nor was a deficient curriculum the only problem faced by the district. For example, because there were so few teachers, each one had to cover all aspects of his or her subject. Thus, North Creek's two science teachers taught general science, earth science, biology, chemistry, and physics. Needless to say, they were not well qualified in all of these.

Perhaps because of these sorts of problems, the district's students scored relatively poorly on standardized tests designed to measure advanced levels of subject-matter knowledge. However, if they weren't exactly the best physics and foreign language students in the state, they certainly weren't the worst. More importantly perhaps, they were well above the state means on tests of basic skills.

Scheduling problems were severe in the high school. This was because many courses could only be offered every other year. If students missed taking a course in the normal year, or if they failed a course and had to take it over, the chances were very good that they would have to wait two years and that it wouldn't fit into their program.

High-quality faculty were hard to recruit and retain in North Creek. Many teachers were unwilling to live and work in the "boonies." This recruiting problem was made worse by the relative poverty of the district; its salaries were among the lowest in Columbia.

These problems, and many others, would be substantially alleviated if North Creek was annexed to Esterville, making a single larger district. It was within Hastings's authority, as commissioner of education, to force such a consolidation if, in his judgment as a professional educator, such an action was the appropriate remedy for the district's deficiencies.

The problem was that neither the students nor the residents of North Creek thought that their schools were particularly deficient. More precisely, while they admitted to many of the problems just noted, they claimed that little schools such as theirs had many virtues, and that these virtues offset their deficiencies. For example, they pointed out that because their schools were so small, virtually all students participated in numerous extracurricular activities. These activities gave them a chance to develop new skills and leadership abilities. Everyone who wanted to play basketball made North Creek's team, and everyone who wanted to write had a place on the school's paper and yearbook. If forced to go to Esterville, many of those opportunities would disappear.

Further, because North Creek's classes were small, teachers got to know students well and could better meet individual needs. Individualization was further abetted by the fact that teachers, parents, and students met each other frequently outside of school in stores, churches, and social events. North Creek students did not suffer from the anomie so prevalent among their counterparts in larger schools. Serious discipline problems were almost nonexistent.

Finally, North Creek School was the center of the community. It served as a site for social and athletic events and was a source of community pride.

Indeed, just the year before the district's marching band had won the state championship in its division and come home to the village's equivalent of a tickertape parade. This sort of unity of school and community would vanish if students were bused to Esterville. Residents were very possessive of their school. They were adamantly opposed to any attempt to merge it with its larger neighbor.

Hastings recognized that small size had certain advantages and that these might be lost if North Creek was merged with Esterville. But the fact remained that because of the inevitable curricular deficiencies of small schools, North Creek's students were getting a lower-quality education than other students in the state. It was Hastings's job to insure that equality of educational opportunity existed in Columbia. And whatever else that phrase might mean, it certainly meant that some children in the state ought not to receive a substandard education merely because they happened to have been born in a small rural village – or merely because they and their parents happened to be satisfied with the school there.

Some Questions

1. Assume the facts of the case are correct, in particular that North Creek students are unable to take many courses that students elsewhere in Columbia can take. Is that a denial of equality of educational opportunity? Why?
2. If you answered "yes" to question 1, consider the following: Suppose there is a very wealthy district in the state of Columbia that offers its students seven different foreign languages, including Urdu. Are the other students in Columbia denied equality of opportunity because they cannot take Urdu?
3. In part, the impending conflict between Commissioner Hastings and the people of North Creek has to do with differing conceptions of student need. The commissioner thinks that students need the better teachers and richer course offerings that would be available to them in Esterville. The people, on the other hand, think that students need the more intimate surroundings of a small school. Who is entitled to decide such questions?
4. Consider the "principle of equal treatment" discussed under "Concept: Equality" earlier in this chapter. How are the students of North Creek and Esterville alike, such that the former should receive the same high school courses as the latter? Is that a question for professionals such as Hastings to decide?

CHAPTER 5

Educational Evaluation

A CASE

"He'll resign for how much?" Paula Carlton could hardly believe her ears. John Corrales, the attorney for Frank Banner, had just proposed that she could have Banner's resignation for the price of a good recommendation to be approved by Corrales and a buyout of Banner's contract for a mere $100,000. "One hundred thousand," Corrales repeated. "You know that if we go to court over this it will cost you more than that. Besides, if you go to court with the case you've got you are going to lose. You'll have spent the money and Frank will still be here."

Paula Carlton's first thought was to throw Corrales out of her office on some appropriate part of his anatomy. The idea that she had to bribe a clearly incompetent teacher to resign and had to favorably recommend him to some other unsuspecting school district to boot was hard to accept. However, she was constrained from depositing Corrales on his posterior in the hall by the fact that he was probably right. The case she had for dismissing Banner was not sound. Moreover, if the district pursued the matter in court, it would be expensive. Quite possibly Corrales's proposal was a good deal for the district.

Frank Banner was one of two tenured teachers at West High whom Paula Carlton considered incompetent. He was also the worst and potentially the most dangerous. From almost the first day she had been on the job as superintendent of the New Delaware School District, she had started to get parental complaints about Banner, who was one of three chemistry teachers at West High. Parents claimed that Banner taught their children nothing, that he knew little about chemistry, and that discipline was nonexistent. By the time she had received her fifth parental complaint, she decided to look into the matter.

She had first called Ben Belnap, West High's principal. He had been distinctly unhelpful. He reported that Banner was not West's best teacher, but that he was certainly not incompetent. As for parents, "they complain about everything." Her next step was to pull Banner's personnel file. Three things stood out. First, Banner's students scored markedly lower on the state's standardized achievement test in chemistry than did the students taught by other teachers at West High. Since the chemistry classes were untracked and used the same curriculum, she could see little that would account for this difference except the quality of instruction.

Second, although Belnap's yearly evaluations of Banner had been unenthusiastic, they were hardly indicative of incompetence. Belnap was required to evaluate each teacher at West on several factors, using a five-point scale on which 5 was excellent and 1 was unsatisfactory. He had given Banner a 2 on discipline and a 2 on classroom management. Other categories such as lesson plans and lesson preparation had rated scores of 3 or 4. At the bottom of the evaluation form in the section for comments he had written, "some areas of performance could use improvement." Looking farther back into the file, she found that Banner had received similar ratings for several years.

The third thing that came to her attention was that the file contained several letters from irate parents, one of which was signed only "a concerned parent." All of these letters accused Banner of gross incompetence. Several also accused him of heavy drinking, although there was no suggestion that he was drinking on the job. Unfortunately, there was no indication that Belnap had taken any steps to check out the substance of the complaints. Nor was there any indication that Belnap had acquainted Banner with the existence of these letters. They had simply gone into Banner's personnel file.

Paula Carlton's next step was to discuss the file and the complaints with Banner. His defense was that he had a different teaching philosophy from the other chemistry teachers at West High. He believed in a nondirective approach to teaching. Moreover, he believed in teaching students to think, not just to regurgitate facts. Of course his students did not do well on the state's tests, but they led on the state test for critical thinking. He pointedly noted that the district had no policy specifying any particular teaching strategy, and it had prided itself in leaving such decisions to the professional judgment of teachers.

This discussion had left Paula Carlton uncertain about what was going on. She decided to pay a surprise visit to Banner's chemistry class. Nothing in the parental complaints or Belnap's evaluations prepared her for what she saw. Banner spent the period apparently teaching chemistry to his desk and the chalk board. It was hard to judge the content of the lesson because it was largely inaudible. She did note that two of the three equations written on the board were incorrect. She was pleased that she remembered some of her college chemistry.

Students in the class ranged from inattentive to positively disruptive. Most were engaged in private conversations. Several others were doing homework for other classes. Most alarmingly, three students were heating a beaker over a bunsen burner, dumping into it spoonfuls of chemicals that were taken, seemingly at random, from jars removed from an unlocked cabinet. Mr. Banner seemed oblivious to this. Paula Carlton wondered if she should check out the school's liability insurance. But the experience was sufficient to convince her that Banner had to go. No student was about to learn chemistry from Banner. They would be lucky to get through the year without blowing themselves up. Banner seemed the teacher the state legislature had in mind when it wrote the law on dismissal for incompetence.

Nevertheless, it was not clear that he could be dismissed for incompetence. His record did not indicate incompetence. Could he be dismissed as a result of one observation and unsubstantiated parental complaints? That was doubtful. Neither could he be left in the class until a defensible case was developed. Could she trust Belnap, the principal, to build a case? He did not seem to take teacher evaluation seriously. Moreover, she was reluctant to leave Banner in the class for that long. He was not only inept; his lack of supervision was dangerous. Perhaps the $100,000 was a small price to pay.

DISPUTE

A: A person is innocent until proven guilty.

B: Sure, that's true in a court of law, but what if you see someone who is obviously incompetent. As an administrator, you have an obligation to protect students from incompetent teachers. Each day lost in a classroom is a precious commodity that can never be reclaimed. You have to be courageous and get rid of incompetence as soon as possible. That's what your job is really about.

A: I'm not against courage or for students losing valuable learning time, but there have to be procedures to protect teachers against arbitrary and unfair administrators, don't there? Without set procedures, administrators could just fire teachers on a whim or because they don't like them or something like that. And that wouldn't be fair.

B: You sound like a union representative! What about being fair to students? Is it fair to put them into a room with a teacher you know can't teach? I know we have procedures for bringing charges of incompetence against teachers, but I am arguing that they are too complicated and time-consuming. They protect the teacher, not the students. We ought to get rid of such procedures and let the administrators do their job. Trust us and give us the power to run good schools, and we'll do it, by God, or you can fire us, too!

A: If you were to be fired, wouldn't you want to know why and on what basis you were being fired?

B: Well, yes.

A: And wouldn't you want to have a chance to defend yourself if any of the negative claims being made about you weren't true?

B: Yes.
A: And if you were told you were incompetent and you thought you were quite competent, wouldn't you demand to compare your evidence of your competence to their evidence of your incompetence?
B: Yes.
A: Then you want to be considered innocent until proven guilty.
B: I sure do!
A: Well??

CONCEPT: DUE PROCESS

The issues in this case concern due process. Paula Carlton has reason to believe that Banner is incompetent. It is less clear, however, that she has evidence that could be defended in court. Nor is it clear that Mr. Banner has been treated fairly. Most of the questions about the adequacy of Paula Carlton's case against Mr. Banner and the fairness of his treatment are issues of due process. Due process is, of course, an important legal concept. But it is also an ethical concept. Here we will be concerned with its moral content.

What is due process? Generally, issues of due process concern the nature of fair procedures for making decisions. The question is: What counts as fairness in making decisions about matters that affect others' lives? Questions of due process are not usually directly concerned with the fairness of the decision itself, but with the fairness of the process used to reach it. It is too much to demand of administrators or of any human being that every decision reached be correct. But we can expect decision makers to take proper care in how they reach their decisions. Due process tells us what counts as taking proper care.

At the core of the concept of due process is the idea of rationality. Rationality requires that equal regard be given to all sides in a case and that all appropriate evidence be brought to bear. What is to be desired in any decision is that it be justified by available evidence, that it be reasonable. Due process defines the kinds of rationally required procedures that will yield reasonable and justified decisions. Conversely, failure to follow due process procedures is usually to fail to take due regard for evidence or for other reasonable requirements for procedural fairness. Rationality is not all that there is to due process, but it is its central element.

Consider some of the features of due process.

One aspect of due process is the idea of notice. If people are to be judged according to the quality of their performances, it is reasonable to claim that they have a right to know the standards according to which they are to be judged. It is unreasonable and unfair to hold people responsible for meeting expectations of which they are ignorant.

This aspect of due process requires that people be judged according to standards that are both known in advance and sufficiently clear that people can know what counts as meeting them. Arguably, this aspect of due process has been violated in Mr. Banner's case. He has been evaluated annually, but these evaluations have given him no reason to believe that his work was unsatisfactory. If the district is now to attempt to dismiss him for doing the same quality of work that he has been doing all along, it is reasonable to accuse the district of lacking consistent public standards for evaluating teachers. Moreover, the district has no policies concerning acceptable teaching methods. They have left such matters up to teachers. Thus Mr. Banner has a reasonable case that he has not been given fair notice of district expectations and a chance to comply with them.

A second aspect of due process is the rational requirement that standards must be consistently applied. Two students who do the same quality of work ought to receive the same grade. Likewise, a teacher whose performance is consistent from year to year ought to receive the same evaluation. Thus, if the district should claim to have some known standard for evaluating teachers, Mr. Banner can claim that this standard was not applied consistently to him. The fact that he received radically different evaluations from Mr. Belnap and from Ms. Carlton indicates that such standards as the district has are capriciously applied.

A third component of due process is that decisions should be made on the basis of reasonable evidence and that procedures should be followed that make such evidence available on a systematic basis. There are a number of things in this case that suggest procedural problems in the collection of evidence. For one, Paula Carlton has based her decision to attempt to dismiss Banner on a single personal visit. But visits from the superintendent are not normally a part of the procedures for evaluating teachers. Nor is one visit sufficient for such a judgment. Moreover, the visit was unannounced. Paula Carlton has not given Mr. Banner a chance to prepare for his evaluation. Arguably, of course, it is more important to discover what teachers normally do than it is to discover what they can do. Nevertheless, unannounced visits are often inconsistent with common practice in teacher evaluation and may be a violation of due process.

Paula Carlton has also relied on standardized test scores to evaluate Mr. Banner. If such test scores are to be fairly used, it must be the case that teachers whose teaching is compared are teaching similar students and are attempting to accomplish similar goals. Paula Carlton has some evidence to believe the former. Students are not tracked into the three sections of chemistry. Yet the quirks of high school scheduling can often generate sections of students of differing ability without a conscious effort at tracking. Perhaps one section of chemistry conflicts with orchestra or with an advanced placement math class. Such things can introduce a selection effect into test scores. Due process requires that if test scores are to be used in evaluating teachers, one must be able to show that differences in scores are due to differences in teaching ability, not to differences in student ability. Moreover, Paula Carlton has reason to believe that the goals of the different chemistry teachers are not identical. If this is true, it may well be the case that the standardized test is less appropriate for Mr. Banner's class.

Finally, the fact that Mr. Belnap has introduced unverified and, in one case, anonymous letters into Mr. Banner's file raises an issue of due process. Unless further steps are taken to verify the parents' complaints, they have the status of hearsay evidence. They are simply unsubstantiated rumor. One of the rules for collecting and judging evidence is that hearsay is not acceptable evidence. Thus complaints about Mr. Banner's teaching should not be part of his file. Especially, they should not be used in making any judgment about his fitness to teach unless they are independently established.

A final feature of the concept of due process is that such standards as are used in judging individuals or their work have to have a rational connection to a legitimate purpose. Paula Carlton has apparently not based her case against Banner on the charge that he is a heavy drinker. Were she to do so she would very likely violate this standard of due process unless she was also able to show that his drinking affected his job performance. Otherwise, the fact that Banner drank, even the fact that he was a heavy drinker, would lack a rational connection to any legitimate purpose of the school.

We observed at the beginning of this discussion that at the core of the idea of due process is the notion of rationality. We have seen in general how this is so and seen that due process has to do primarily with ensuring that reasonable decisions are made about other people in a rationally justified way using adequate evidence. Let us now consider more directly how these various aspects of due process connect to rationality and the adequacy and reliability of evidence.

Often due process standards are simply procedures for collecting and evaluating evidence. The notion that hearsay evidence is an unacceptable basis for making a decision about a person, for example, is based on the view that rumors, opinions expressed by people who are not expert about some matter, or testimony by people who are biased or not known to be reliable observers are suspect as evidence. Rationality demands that evidence from such sources should be disregarded or independently checked. The evidence provided by parents in this case should be regarded as hearsay. The point is not that parents are somehow particularly stupid or dishonest. Possibly much of what they have said will check out. At the same time, they have not been in a position to observe Mr. Banner's class, they are not expert about chemistry or teaching, and they must also rely for much of their information on their children. Moreover, since their children are not doing well in Mr. Banner's class, they may be biased. There is thus much reason to be cautious about the reliability of their views.

Many other features of due process are also designed to generate reliable evidence. In proceedings in which a suspension or termination is possible, administrators are required to provide a hearing in which evidence is checked and witnesses are cross-examined. The point of such a hearing is to provide an opportunity to check the reliability of the evidence on which a decision is based. When the decision is particularly important, elaborate procedures may be required. Again, the point is not to make the decision more complex or to harbor incompetents. It is to ensure that important matters are decided on the basis of reliable evidence.

The emphasis on judging people according to known and clear standards has a similar connection to rationality. Reasonable judgments require some standard of judgment. For example, an administrator who lacks a clear view of what counts as good teaching cannot make a reasoned decision about whether a particular instance of teaching is good. Nor can teachers make a reasonable attempt to follow the standard if it is unknown or is so unclear that it is impossible to know what counts as meeting it. Moreover, a rational judgment of a teacher's ability cannot be made if the teacher does not know what is expected. Rational decision making is thus impossible in the absence of clear standards.

Finally, the demand that standards be consistently applied expresses a demand for rational decision making. Here the argument is identical to that made in the previous chapter for the claim that equals must be treated equally. If two teachers, Jones and Smith, perform identically on the appropriate standard, any argument for giving Jones a certain benefit contingent on that performance will also be an argument for giving the same benefit to Smith. A procedure that assigns different benefits to teachers who have performed similarly is, therefore, not only unjust, but irrational.

In essence, then, due process requires administrators to make reasonable decisions by following rational procedures that generate reliable evidence and consistent judgments. Generally, the extensiveness of the effort required to generate reliable evidence should be proportional to the seriousness of the interest affected.

ANALYSIS: RESPECT FOR PERSONS

In previous chapters we have tried to show how the concepts we have dealt with can be interpreted within the context of different ethical theories. We have looked at consequentialist theories, for which the principle of benefit maximization is primary, and nonconsequentialist theories, for which the principle of respect for persons is primary. We have tried to be evenhanded in our presentation, although the astute reader may have detected a higher level of enthusiasm for nonconsequentialist views. Here we want to argue for the primacy of the value of respect for persons. The point of our argument is not that the principle of benefit maximization has no role in ethical thought. It is, rather, that it should be subordinate to the principle of equal respect. It will be convenient to argue this here because the principles of due process seem to fit most comfortably into a nonconsequentialist framework.

Why give people due process? Given the discussion above, the question is tantamount to asking why people should be treated reasonably. For someone for whom the principle of benefit maximization is primary, the answer must be that the consequences of treating people reasonably are better than those of treating people unreasonably. If teachers are evaluated capriciously, for example, they may be denied some benefit, such as tenure or a merit-pay raise, causing them to become discouraged and not try to perform better. Reasonable treatment, it would seem, produces better consequences than unreasonable treatment.

No doubt this is true. Yet we can reasonably ask if it is really necessary, in order to show that we should treat people reasonably, to prove that some type of benefit would be maximized. What about cases in which no benefit is achieved in treating someone reasonably? Isn't it possible to argue that we simply should treat people reasonably because it is our moral responsibility to do so? Isn't treating others reasonably a part of our making morally responsible decisions and a part of respecting the value of others? Suppose that we could point to some situations in which unreasonable treatment did no harm and reasonable treatment produced no good. Should unreasonable treatment be condoned? Consider, for example, another area that often raises issues of due process: grading. Suppose that a teacher capriciously assigned a particular grade to a student in a high school class. But suppose also that nothing turned on the grade. Perhaps the student had already been admitted to college, thus rendering the capricious grade harmless. Would it then be morally acceptable to assign the grade on an entirely arbitrary basis? Could we toss a term paper down the stairs and assign a grade on the basis of which step the paper landed on? No harm—no foul?

One response to this question is that some harm inevitably results. The student who has been graded capriciously will inevitably feel wronged. He or she may resent the teacher or become alienated from the subject matter or education generally. Thus there is harm done. But such a response is, at its heart, a nonconsequentialist one. If no benefit is at stake, why should the student feel wronged by being graded capriciously? In fact, from the consequentialist point of view, if no benefit is at stake, the student has not been wronged. Or if he or she has been wronged, the wrong consists in the fact that arbitrary treatment denies the student equal respect. If the student *justifiably* feels wronged, it is because the capricious treatment is an affront to the student's dignity and worth, not because he or she has lost some benefit. The other harms result from the initial feelings of having been treated unfairly. They are only harms if this initial reaction about being unjustly treated is warranted. It appears, then, that the principle of equal respect is central to the notion of due process in a way that the principle of benefit maximization is not.

Moreover, approaching issues of due process through the principle of benefit maximization often produces odd results. Consider the matter of discipline and punishment. One important moral concept about punishment is that the punishment should fit the crime. Generally, the idea seems to be that people who have done something morally wrong deserve to suffer in proportion to the evil they have done. Too much punishment or too little is inappropriate. This conception of punishment makes sense from the nonconsequentialist point of view, because it recognizes that people are morally responsible for their choices and that they can do evil. It recognizes that people are sometimes guilty. And it provides a way to absolve guilt through punishment. One justly suffers proportionately to the wrong one has done.

Consequentialists have considerable difficulty in explaining why punishment should fit the crime. For the consequentialist, punishment, if it is appropriate at all, must be justified by its consequences. Deterrence of further misbehavior is typical of the desirable consequences thought to result from punishment. But how much punishment is enough if the point of punishment is to deter? The answer, of course, is that the punishment required is that which is enough to discourage people from misbehaving. But there is no special reason to assume that such punishment as is sufficient to deter will also fit the crime.

Chewing gum is a common school "crime." Its punishment is normally a modest reprimand or a brief detention: trivial punishments for a trivial infraction. It is obvious to any teacher that these punishments do not deter. Students continue to chew gum. We propose that if gum chewers were to be hung from the school flagpole, gum chewing would quickly cease. Indeed, once the policy was announced (assuming it was believed), we suspect that gum chewing would cease immediately, relieving the administrator of the unpleasant duty of executing any bubble-gum malefactors. Nevertheless, the suggestion seems highly offensive. Presumably that is because the punishment is radically inappropriate to the offense. It is, however, difficult for the nonconsequentialist to explain why the solution is inappropriate if it works.

Nonconsequentialist views also provide more plausible accounts of due process. We are obligated to treat people reasonably because they are people. Treating people reasonably respects them as persons. Capricious treatment denies the worth of the person maltreated.

It is important here to return to the concept of persons as moral agents. Persons are free and rational moral agents who are responsible for their choices and who have the duty to choose wisely. Presumably part of what we mean by the idea of responsible and wise choice is that decisions will be made reasonably on the basis of evidence. Respect not only for persons, but also for reasoned decisions, thus seems central to the nonconsequentialist view. To treat others capriciously seems not only to fail to show them equal respect, but is to act in a way that is inconsistent with one's own status as a free and rational moral agent.

We want to offer two additional arguments for a nonconsequentialist viewpoint. First, it seems that the principle of benefit maximization may presuppose something very like the principle of equal respect. Most human beings value their own happiness and their own welfare. But why should they value the happiness and welfare of others? Note that the principle of benefit maximization requires people to value the welfare of others equally with their own. It requires of us, not that we act so as to maximize our own welfare, but that we act so as to maximize the average welfare. Indeed, the principle of benefit maximization can require an individual to act against his or her own welfare because the average welfare requires it. According to the principle of benefit maximization, everyone's happiness or everyone's welfare counts equally. But why should this be so? Why should we be concerned about anyone else's welfare? Or why should we care more about the welfare of human beings than cows? Here, while other answers are possible, it is very tempting to appeal to the idea of respect for persons. We should care about the happiness or welfare of others as well as our own because they, like us, are persons. Their interests and their welfare are equally as important as our own. Such a response is surely attractive and plausible, but to give it is to make the principle of benefit maximization subordinate to the principle of equal respect. In short, it is to grant the point that we are arguing. The principle of equal respect for persons is morally basic. Other principles are justified in its terms and are subordinate to it.

A final argument has to do with the concepts of happiness and growth. It is one that should be particularly appealing to educators. Consider that a nonconsequentialist view places a premium on the capacity for reflective, rational choice. Recognizing that people are free moral agents, its central concern is that this capacity for rational choice should be exercised responsibly. However, neither the capacity for free choice nor the skills and attitudes for its responsible exercise are present at birth. Infants do not choose, they respond to stimuli. The growth of the capacity for free and responsible choice is a difficult and complex topic. It would be possible to engage in a long discussion of how or even if it is possible. We make two assumptions. First, growth as a moral agent is possible, and the process of becoming a moral agent involves learning and education. Second, educators are in the business of creating responsible moral agents. Indeed, we believe that it is their central task.

Suppose, however, that happiness was possible apart from moral growth. Consider a rather imaginative but, we hope, forceful example. Imagine that in some future time a group of scientists announced that they had discovered a way to make all of humanity infinitely and permanently happy. All that was necessary was for people to turn themselves in to a hospital where they would have electrodes implanted in their brains that would stimulate their pleasure centers at appropriate intervals. Since they would be blissfully unaware of anything except their own pleasure, they would be fed intravenously and would be confined to the hospital bed for the rest of their days. People need not be concerned about this, however, because the advance of robotics and automation have made the economy self-sufficient, self-regulating, and fool-proof. Human beings need be concerned about nothing beyond their own happiness. Indeed, once they were wired in, they would need to be concerned about nothing. Concern itself would be a thing of the past. The mind would be given over entirely to the experience of happiness.

This thought experiment proposes a trade. It asks whether we would be willing to exchange the use and development of our faculties, those faculties of reflection and choice that mark us as persons, for a life of guaranteed and unending happiness. Our moral sensitivities rebel against such a proposal. We expect most readers will agree. But what is the basis of such a response? Here it is easy for a nonconsequentialist to respond. The proposal requires us to abandon everything that is morally central to a responsible human life. It is not an acceptable exchange. It is not clear what a consequentialist (at least one for whom the good to be maximized is happiness) could say. The thought experiment stipulates that happiness is maximized. What else counts?

CONCLUSION

Socrates is recorded as saying that the unexamined life is not worth living. Why not? In our view, the point of this maxim is that to fail to reflect on how one lives is to fail to recognize one's status as a moral agent. It is to refuse to be responsible for one's self. In a fundamental way, it is to refuse to be a person. We have been unhappy with consequentialism because for consequentialists it is happiness or human welfare, not growth as persons, that is central. Growth for the consequentialist is a contingent value. It is a matter of interest only when it leads to happiness.

In our view, growth as a moral agent, as someone who cares about others and is willing and able to accept responsibility for one's self, is the compelling matter. Promoting this kind of development is what teachers and administrators ought to be fundamentally about, whatever else it is that they are about. As educators, we are first and foremost in the business of creating persons.

ADDITIONAL CASES

A Letter of Recommendation

September 23, 1986

Mr. John Sitallsky
Superintendent, York School District
1301 West Avenue
York, New Hampshire 90814

Dear John:

Your letter arrived yesterday, and it was good to hear from you. I hope things are settling down. From your description, York sounds like a damned difficult district. A superintendency is a tough job under any conditions. When it's your first one, and you've got a board the likes of York's, it can be awful. Hang in there. You remember my first year at Westville, when you were principal out at Hammond School. That was my first job as a chief school officer, and I thought I'd never make it through the year. I've always appreciated the support you gave me in that difficult period.

Anyway, you asked about Carol Miller. I'll tell you what I can, but my memory may be a little hazy on some of the details. It's been almost five years, and since I'm no longer in Westville, her records aren't available to me. Be sure to get them from the personnel folks there, so that you can check on my recollections of her performance.

Mrs. Miller came to the district in the Spring of 1977 to fill in for my regular home economics teacher, who went on maternity leave. As I recall, she was highly recommended by her professors at State. Initially, I'd planned to keep her only until the end of the school year, because I expected Mrs. Woodwall (the regular home ec teacher) to return to the classroom in September. When Woodwall decided at the last minute to stay home and raise her kid, I was stuck, so I kept Miller on.

All in all, it was a good choice. I don't recall exactly how many times I observed her classroom, probably two or three, but I do remember that she always struck me as being well prepared and as taking an interest in her work. I very definitely recall her capacity to motivate her students, especially the boys—most of whom didn't want to be in a home economics course. She was, I think, a damned good home ec teacher. Certainly better than Woodwall.

I also remember appointing Miller to head up a curriculum revision committee during her third year at Westville. I had occasion to work with her directly then, and I remember that she impressed me as being thoroughly trained in her field. As far as subject matter competence goes, she's probably as good as you're going to get.

On the downside, there's the matter of her attendance. At least while I was running Westville, I could count on her to use every sick day, personal day, and professional day she had coming. I could also count on her to cash them in on Mondays. Every administrator knows that teachers tend to get sick on Fridays and Mondays, but Miller must've set a record in that regard. Be sure and check on this matter with whoever's personnel director in Westville these days.

A pattern of absences is important to recognize, but it's more important to know why it occurs. Maybe Miller just happens to catch colds on Mondays. I don't believe that for a minute, but it's possible. Perhaps, like most of the others who pull this stunt, she just wanted more long weekend vacations than the school calendar offers. I'd give that explanation a "definite maybe." What makes me doubt it is that she only missed work on Mondays, not Fridays and Mondays (which, you'll soon discover, is the usual pattern of the long weekenders on your faculty).

What I heard was that she and her husband hit the bottle pretty hard on weekends, and they needed Mondays to sober up. Now, I don't know that for a fact, of course. But I met her husband's boss once at a Kiwanis meeting, and he (the boss) complained of the same pattern of absence in Miller's spouse. He said that he knew the Millers very well socially and that they were both "a couple of lushes." His words. He claimed that their drinking was the reason neither one could make it to work on Mondays.

I'd try to clear this up, if I were you. I think Mrs. Miller's a pretty good teacher. I'd hire her, if it weren't for the absenteeism. Even with it, I might employ her, if I could be sure that she just likes to take her vacations in three-day chunks. (I'd certainly sit down with her beforehand and have a little heart-to-heart about where I expected her to be on Mondays. But I'd probably hire her.) However, if she's into the sauce so heavily that she needs to take a day off every couple of weeks to recover, I wouldn't touch her with the proverbial ten-foot pole. There's too much at stake. We can't risk having an alkie running a classroom, especially a home ec classroom, where there's always the risk of a serious accident. The teacher really has to be alert in those situations, not hung over.

Well, that's about all I can tell you about Carol Miller. Best of luck in the new job, and give my regards to Helen and the kids.

Sincerely,

Charles L. Kaufmann,
Superintendent
Polk County School District

Some Questions

1. Has Kaufmann behaved unethically? That is, does reporting hearsay evidence in a letter of recommendation count as behaving unethically?
2. If you answered "yes" to the previous question, how could Kaufmann fulfill his responsibility to provide an accurate recommendation and alert his colleague to what is potentially a very serious problem? Sketch out such a letter.
3. Presumably the heavy use of alcohol or other drugs by a teacher is relevant information for judging that teacher's fitness for the classroom. Also presumably, most teachers who abuse alcohol or drugs will not volunteer that fact to prospective or current employers. How then are school administrators to gain such information without violating a teacher's rights to privacy and due process?
4. We have said in this chapter's opening case study that to consider heavy drinking in a performance evaluation would be a violation of a teacher's due process rights unless it is also shown that the drinking affects his or her job performance. Short of the teacher's being "falling-down drunk" in the classroom or something equally obvious, isn't such a matter impossible to prove? If you think it is possible, describe how you would do it.
5. Administrators sometimes argue that it is okay to "cut corners" on matters such as a teacher's due process rights *if* the purpose is to benefit the school. Is it okay? Would a consequentialist and a nonconsequentialist answer this question differently?

A Matter of Standards

Charles Brick was troubled. As principal of Eastview High School, it was his responsibility to make recommendations regarding the appointment and tenure of his faculty to the district's superintendent. He was not sure what he should recommend regarding the reappointment of Lillian Wilson. More to the point, he was not sure how he could reasonably decide what to recommend.

Lillian was in her third year as an American history teacher at Eastview. As a consequence, she would either be awarded tenure or released at the end of the current term. In deciding which of these two courses of action to take, the principal always relied heavily on his department chair's judgment. Brick realized that as an ex-physical education teacher, he was not as good a judge of the subject-matter competence as the department head in that subject.

The problem was that Chesterton School District required that probationary teachers be evaluated by two department chairpersons during their first three years. On the surface, this policy made sense. It was supposed to insure that another perspective was brought to bear in the evaluation process and thereby insure that beginners' careers were not dependent on the perceptions of a single person. Thus Wilson had been evaluated by Charlie Tomkins, the head of the social studies department, three times during her probationary period at Eastview. But she had also been evaluated by Rita Morales, the social studies chairperson at Roosevelt High School, an equal number of times during the same period. And these evaluations, in accordance with district policy, had been carried out quite independently of each other.

The district's teacher evaluation form provided a series of scales for observers to use in judging a teacher's competence. Various instructional criteria were to be rated on a five-point scale, from "outstanding" to "below average." For example, the observation instrument required observers to rate the following items:

> *Discipline:* Does the teacher maintain control of the class at all times? Are disciplinary procedures fair? Describe.
>
> *Individual Differences:* Does the teacher adapt his or her instruction to take account of individual differences among pupils? Give examples.
>
> *Lesson Objectives:* Were lesson objectives made clear to pupils? Describe.

The problem arose because Morales's and Tomkins's evaluations were in nearly total disagreement. Morales had given Wilson "outstanding" on several of the rating scales and "above average" on all of the remainder. She had strongly recommended Wilson's reappointment. On the other hand, the highest rating given to Wilson by Tomkins was "average." He had rated her "below average" on several of the criteria, and he had recommended against tenure. It was hard for Brick to imagine a more disparate set of evaluations.

What was even more astonishing was that Morales and Tomkins had apparently observed much the same behavior on Wilson's part. For example, under the item concerning individual differences, Morales had written:

> Excellent. Teacher had collected a variety of books on the same topic that required different levels of reading skill. These books were readily at hand during the lesson, and they were assigned to students according to their reading competence. I also noted that she varied the complexity of the explanations she gave according to student ability.

On the other hand, Tomkins had written in response to the same question:

> Below average. Teacher relies heavily on books to individualize instruction, but the same basic lesson was taught to the entire class. While attempts were seemingly made to vary the level of discourse in the classroom, these must be faulted because attempts to simplify explanations often resulted in oversimplified, even incorrect, remarks.

In an attempt to reach some sort of justified conclusion regarding Wilson's competence, Brick had called Morales and Tomkins into his office to discuss their evaluations. That had not helped at all. In fact, all it seemed to accomplish was to make the two department heads distrustful of each other's competence. The two had ended up arguing over vague and (to Brick's mind) largely irrelevant aspects of educational philosophy.

Brick was unsure how to proceed, and his recommendation to the superintendent was due in less than a week.

Some Questions

1. We have said that due process requires that standards be sufficiently clear that people can know what counts as meeting them. Consider the standards involved in this case—namely, those for discipline, individual differences, and lesson objectives. Do these meet the clarity standard required for due process? Why or why not?
2. If you answered "no" to the previous question, can you write suitably clear standards for these matters? Write one for classroom discipline. If you have difficulty doing so, what does this say—in principle—about meeting due process standards in teacher evaluation?
3. Why not bring in a "tie-breaker"? That is, what would be ethically dubious about getting another social studies chairperson to come in to observe Wilson and make a recommendation to Brick?
4. Most school districts do not have the double evaluation system described in this case—that is, with department heads from two schools carrying out evaluations of probationary teachers. Is having two separate evaluators a good idea? Consider this policy in the light of the consistency standard of due process.
5. In education, one standard approach to the problem of vague criteria is to break down global requirements into highly specific ones. Writing "behavioral objectives" for student evaluations is an example. What might be wrong, from a due process perspective, with this approach to teacher evaluation?

A Problem of Grades

The meeting with the parents of the students in Mrs. Milner's high-track junior English class had gone smoothly enough. No individuals had lost their composure. There had been no overt belligerence. Still, Janet McDonald, the principal of Washington High, had no clear idea of what she would do about the matter.

The complaints were about Mrs. Milner's grading. She seemed to view the teaching of American literature roughly in the way a drill sergeant viewed recruits' initiation into the Marine Corps. A mixture of toughness and capriciousness was seen as a virtue. Mrs. Milner was young. In fact, it was her first year. She would learn that excellence and maintaining standards were not synonymous with mindless discipline and vicious grading. But that would be too late for this year's students. Janet McDonald hoped that the students' willingness to read good literature would recover from their experience. She was more concerned about miseducation than misgrading.

Parents had raised four issues. First, the average in Mrs. Milner's college preparatory class was substantially lower than those in the other sections taught by other teachers. Yet these other sections had the same curriculum and students of similar ability. The average in Mrs. Milner's class was a feeble C , while that of other classes was B. Parents pointed out that English grades were crucial in college admissions. Many of the students wanted to enter highly selective schools. Poor grades in junior English could make a substantial difference, not only because a C − did not look good on a transcript, but because it unfairly lowered a student's rank in class compared to pupils in other sections who were doing the same quality of work.

Second, Mrs. Milner used what the parents called a "fudge factor" in her grading. A fourth of the grade was based on what she called "class performance." Most students seemed to think that class performance was equivalent to bootlicking. Students who stayed after class and expressed their undying love of *Moby Dick* and *The Scarlet Letter* inevitably did well in this aspect of their grades.

Third, Mrs. Milner used grades for discipline. She had a system of "errors." Students got an error for such things as being late for class, chewing gum, and talking. Parents thought that these things were unrelated to students' performance in English.

Finally, Mrs. Milner's grading of essays seemed highly subjective, if not downright capricious. Parents had brought in some copies of exams and essays. Janet McDonald had to admit that she was often unsure what Mrs. Milner's questions asked. Further, comments and grades on the essays seemed capricious. The teacher seemed able to overlook a glaring ineptitude in sentence construction while objecting to a plausible interpretation of literary material.

Janet McDonald wondered if Mrs. Milner wasn't punishing students for not accepting her views on a story or novel.

The principal largely agreed with the parents' complaints. Moreover, she wanted to do something. In her experience, capricious grading was a major source of parent grievances and student alienation. But what to do? It was difficult to confront Mrs. Milner with the matter. Principals were supposed to support their teachers, at least publicly, against parents, weren't they? Moreover, Janet McDonald couldn't introduce the problem into Mrs. Milner's regular teacher evaluation. That would be to evaluate her on the basis of hearsay evidence. She could not personally verify much of what parents had told her. Finally, it was difficult to deal with the matter by means of a school policy on grading. Washington High did not have such a policy, because in its principal's experience such policies were either so vague as to be unenforceable or so rigid as to cause more problems than they solved. Perhaps getting the faculty to consider such a policy might help to sensitize them to the inadequacy of their current practices. But for this year that wouldn't help rescue junior English students from Mrs. Milner's clutches.

Some Questions

1. Clearly, it will be a relatively simple matter for McDonald to call in Milner and clear up the matter of grading before the next year's crop of students enroll in junior English. What is she to do, however, about the grades Milner has already awarded?
2. We have said that school grading policies are often "either so vague as to be unenforceable or so rigid as to cause more problems than they solved." Why should that be the case?
3. As an exercise in policy making, try your hand at writing a grading policy for a high school. What would be desirable attributes for such a policy?
4. We have said earlier that standards for judging individuals or their work should "have a rational connection to a legitimate purpose." In this case parents object to using grades as disciplinary tools, arguing that they should only reflect mastery of English. Argue the opposite view, that is, that lowering or raising a student's grade because of classroom behavior is a legitimate act and not inherently a violation of due process.
5. Do you think that a student's effort should be considered when a grade is awarded? That is, if a student tries very hard but does poor work, do you think the student should be given a passing grade? (Perhaps a low one, but passing nonetheless.) If so, how is this different from considering classroom behavior when awarding grades?
6. What purposes do grades serve? How might different answers to this question affect your view of fair procedures for assigning grades?

CHAPTER 6

Educational Authority

A CASE

Fred Cantor sat blinking. If he had heard right, his faculty had just voted down the board of education. And they had elected him to communicate their decision to the board. He had always regarded himself as a democratic administrator, but he was not sure that this was his idea of democracy.

Fred Cantor, the principal of South Elementary, did seek to be democratic. Faculty in his school had a considerable role in decision making. Issues were talked out and some consensus reached. Fred never imposed his views on his faculty. He saw himself as a facilitator and a colleague—a first among equals.

His troubles began with the new curriculum in moral education. At a faculty meeting discussion of the problems of drug abuse, alcohol, and teenage pregnancy, someone had gotten the idea that the school should build character and teach the processes of critical moral judgment. After all, how better could we help the kids in our school to face responsibly these pressing real issues in their lives? Everyone, even Fred, had agreed that this was a good idea. Fred appointed a faculty committee to develop a curriculum. They had done so. The faculty discussed the new curriculum; it was revised in the light of the discussion and implemented. Then the troubles began.

Several parents objected strenuously to the way the new program was being implemented. What the teachers saw as promoting the students' capacity for critical moral thought, these parents saw as undermining their authority. They claimed that the program failed to recognize any moral absolutes. It taught relativism. It was anti-God and anti-American. It had to go. There was talk of the First Amendment and of lawyers.

So the complaining parents went to the school board. They presented their case. The school board listened to them carefully and gave the teachers an opportunity to present their views. The teachers were careful to note that aspects of the program they had implemented were used elsewhere, that it was based on careful research, and that it was, in their expert judgment, just what children needed. The board discussed the matter and voted the program down.

The board's justification for the decision focused heavily on the parents' complaint that the program was inconsistent with their religious convictions. The board expressed its appreciation for the teachers' concern and hard work. It expressed its admiration for the quality of the program and the expertise that it represented. But it said that the religious scruples of its citizens came first. Thus the program was voted out.

The teachers were outraged. At the next teachers' meeting there was a full-scale rebellion against the board. The teachers were generally of the opinion that the purpose of the board of education was to approve budgets, construct buildings, and pay their salaries. They were, after all, laypersons. They knew nothing about education. Educational decisions should be made by the experts—that is, teachers. That the board had stuck its nose into the curriculum and had reversed their considered professional judgment was intolerable.

Fred Cantor was, of course, sympathetic. But what was he supposed to do? Unfortunately, the teachers had an answer. They had proceeded to draft a response to the board stating their views on the merits of the program and on the proper way to run a school district. It contained one memorable passage: "When a board of education exceeds its authority by interfering with the professional judgment of its teachers and administrators, our concern for the welfare of our students and our professional integrity compel us to disobey. We cannot acquiesce in this tyranny over the collective judgment of the professional staff." The statement was unanimously adopted. Fred had been requested to deliver this declaration of independence to the King Georges of the school board. He, however, was not feeling very Jeffersonian. He wondered if his faculty had the right to commit his life and his sacred honor to the task.

DISPUTE

A: Democracy simply means following the will of the people. Their will is expressed through the democratic process of one person, one vote. By committing ourselves to democracy, we commit ourselves to peacefully following the will of the majority even if we are outvoted. That is what democracy is all about.

B: Do you mean that if the majority votes to segregate an ethnic group or, God forbid, exterminate them, I would have to take part in or condone such things?

A: Of course not! Things like that are forbidden by our Constitution. Certain rights to life, liberty, and the pursuit of happiness are basic to democracy and cannot be voted out. Still, voting is the only fair way to give everybody a voice in decision making. Otherwise, you are at the mercy of the arbitrary decision making of anyone in authority.

B: But isn't that just what happens in our democracy? We elect a president,

sure, but once in office, the president can make some very crucial decisions that a majority of the people might disagree with, and there is
nothing you can do about it. Or take a school board. Once they are
elected, they make decisions on the basis of hearing a few irate parents at
meetings and not by asking the community to vote on things again.

A: You are confused and understandably so, because democracy is more
complicated than it first seems. By their vote, the people delegate their
authority to a president or to a school board. The people vote their
confidence in those they elect to make the best judgments they can while
following the democratic procedures associated with their office. A school
board, for example, votes on issues and it itself is democratic.

B: But aren't there some things the board doesn't know enough about to vote
intelligently on, like which reading or math series best fits with the
predominant student characteristics in the community? There are things
that ought to be left to the experts. You call in a nurse or a doctor to
ascertain if a child's rash is measles or an allergy, don't you? You don't take
a vote on it! Even in a democracy, some decisions should be based on
knowledge and not on vote.

A: Granted, but especially in education, it isn't easy to get agreement among
the experts and so the board should have the last say.

B: But you began by saying democracy requires following the will of the
majority. Suppose a 7-member board receives a school faculty vote of 40
to 3 to rescind a board policy? Who is the majority and whose will should
be served and what is the will of the people?

A: I said democracy was complicated, didn't I?

B: No, you said it was simply following the will of the people as expressed by
their vote.

CONCEPT: DEMOCRACY

In our society almost everyone believes in democracy. It is less clear that
everyone agrees on what democracy is or what it requires. In this case Fred
Cantor believes in democracy. He seems to feel that this requires him to allow
his teachers to participate in decision making. The teachers also believe in
democracy. They even appear to believe that they can vote down their board of
education. And the board of education believes in democracy. It believes that it
has the right to decide matters of educational policy because it has been elected
by a majority of the citizens of the district. This conflict stems from too much
democracy.

Yet democracy is not uniformly popular. Some of South Elementary's
parents seem to feel that their rights are being violated. They appear to think

that they have these rights no matter what is democratically decided. Moreover, the teachers seem to believe that while democracy should prevail in their deliberations, it is their expertise that should prevail against the democratic decisions of the board. To sort out these matters we need to address three questions. What is democracy? What are its limits? Why should we accept it?

What is democracy? Because *democracy* is an honorific term, there is a tendency to apply it to any political institution or procedure of governance of which we approve. Here we shall view democracy narrowly as only having to do with decision making. A democratic society or a democratic school, for the purposes of our discussion, then will be one in which decisions are made in a certain way. Our task will be to explore the conditions of democratic decision making.

The following are two of the most basic features of democratic decision making. A decision is made democratically if:

1. The interests of each individual are fairly considered.
2. Each individual has a fair influence on the decision.

Each feature is required. The second feature is required because the first, by itself, is consistent with a benevolent despotism. That is, it is possible to imagine a society in which an enlightened dictator looked out for the interests of everyone. Such a society would not be democratic because it denied participation to people who were entitled to participate in decisions.

The first feature is required because the second, by itself, is consistent with a tyrannical majority. It is possible to imagine a society that governs its affairs by majority rule, but where the majority refuses to respect the legitimate interests of the minority. We would not, for example, be willing to consider as democratic a society where the majority voted to enslave the minority, even if it continued to permit them to vote.

The intuitive idea captured by these basic features is that democracy is a way of making decisions that takes equality seriously. Everyone's interests are to be fairly considered, and everyone has to have a fair chance to affect decisions.

We tend to associate democracy with elections and voting. These, however, are not necessarily required. Democratic decisions may result from discussion and the formation of a consensus. No vote need be taken. Moreover, a decision can fail to be democratic even though elections and voting are involved. Some people may be unfairly excluded from participation in the vote. Or, once elected, officials may serve their own interests rather than the interests of the people. Such practices are undemocratic. We associate elections and voting with democracy because we believe that these practices promote equal participation and equal consideration of interests.

Obviously, however, not everyone is entitled to participate in every decision in a democracy. Voters who live in New York have no reason to complain
if they cannot participate in school board elections in California. Two ideas are
commonly suggested concerning who is entitled to participate. One holds that
people are entitled to a say about some decision if it affects them. The other is
that people are entitled to participate in a decision if they belong to the
community to whom the decision belongs. Both ideas seem to us to have
merit. Neither is sufficient by itself.

It is important to note that in our case there are two communities involved. One is the professional staff of the school, the teachers and the administration. The other is the community of citizens living in the district and their
elected board of education. One issue raised by the case is which community is
the relevant one to make decisions about education. Those who advocate the
democratic operation of schools often seem to mean that schools should be
operated with high levels of participation by teachers in decision making. They
argue for this by claiming that teachers need to be treated as professionals, not
mere employees to be dictated to by management. It is not often realized,
however, that such claims for democratically run schools also tend to exclude
the larger community from decision making about matters of education. To
the extent that teachers have decision-making power over education, the community does not. The issue then becomes one of sovereignty. It is not a
question of how much freedom teachers will be allowed in their professional
lives or of whether it is desirable to delegate decisions. The question is, given a
disagreement, who is entitled to decide. Should the teachers in Fred Cantor's
school be allowed to overrule the school board? Is the claim that teachers are
professionals a reason why teachers, and not elected representatives of the
community, should be entitled to make educational decisions?

This question of sovereignty appears to be what is at issue in our case. The
teachers in Fred Cantor's school have taken to heart his views about the
desirability of democratic schools run by professionals. Why, then, should they
not vote down the board? And why should they not see Fred Cantor as their
representative to the board rather than as the representative of the board's
authority over them?

The tension that exists between the desire to operate schools as democratic
communities and the authority of the school board is often disguised by the
fact that teachers deal with administrators, not school boards. The question,
then, often seems to be whether the principal should share authority with the
teachers or whether the principal should retain authority. To the extent that
this is the question, then the case for democratic schools is strong. Why should
democracy not triumph over administrative tyranny? But this may not be the
question. The administrator's authority in the school is delegated authority.
The administrator represents the authority of the board of education. The

board represents the authority of the electorate. The administrator who de-
cides to run a democratic school may, therefore, be subverting the authority of
the board. And that authority is democratic authority.

Much of what we have said about democracy thus far runs counter to the
teachers' view. The education of the children in a community affects the
welfare of everyone. We all have an interest in good education. Moreover,
those with the most legitimate interest in education are the children and their
parents, not teachers. When we ask what the relevant community is for
educational decision making, it is the larger community, the one represented
by the school board. To take the teachers' side against the board in this case
would appear to violate our second rule for democratic decision making. It
would be to exclude the members of the community whose interests are at
stake from participation in the decision. If educational decisions should be
made democratically, it is difficult to see why they should be made by teachers.

There is, however, more to the issue. Perhaps not all decisions should be
made democratically. This case involves two claims to this effect. The first has
been made implicitly by those parents who have argued that their right to
religious liberty has been violated. These parents are holding that the school
has encroached on their private sphere in that it has challenged the religious
teaching the children have received in the home. We want to agree with two
aspects of the parents' argument. First, the rights of individuals, those things
that are part of the private sphere, are limits on democratic authority. A
violation of someone's rights is no less a violation of rights because people vote
on it. Because we believe in democracy, we need not believe that everything
can be democratically decided. Second, we want to agree that religion is a
private matter. A person's religion is not something over which the government
should have power.

These comments do not decide the issue, however. In this case the school
has not required anyone to accept any religious doctrine or engage in any
religious exercise. What has happened is that the school has proposed to teach
something that is itself nonreligious in its character but that some parents see as
inconsistent with their religious convictions. We assume that the conflict with
the parents' religious belief is real. At the same time, if conflict with someone's
religious convictions was sufficient to remove something from the curriculum
of the public schools, it is questionable as to whether there would be much
curriculum left. Here we leave it to the reader to decide the conditions under
which conflict between some part of the secular curriculum and someone's
religious beliefs would be a sufficient reason for removing something from the
curriculum.

Nevertheless, the school board has refused to permit the program in moral
education, giving as their reason that some parents are offended by it. The staff
of Fred Cantor's school has argued that this decision is objectionable because it

conflicts with the professional opinion of teachers. Is this a potentially successful line of argument? That is, can democratic authority be rightfully limited
when it conflicts with the professional judgment of experts?

Consider a possible argument for limiting democratic authority in this
case. We once heard a story about a teacher who, having heard an inservice
lecture on the virtues of democracy in the classroom, asked the members of
her class to vote on the location of Rome. The class democratically put Rome
in France. Obviously something went wrong. But what? We suggest that the
problem is that the teacher asked the class to determine the truth of some idea
democratically. But truth is not democratic. The truth of the sentence "Rome is
in Italy" is not affected by any vote. It is only affected by the location of Rome.
Fred Cantor's teachers might argue something analogous about the school
board's rejection of their program in moral education. Whether or not this
program is a good program is not affected by any vote. That the program is an
effective one is a question to be decided by experts. Lay boards of education are
not in a position to know what the research says. Nor are they in a position to
evaluate the judgment of professionals. It is the professional staff of the school
who are the educational experts. Thus they are the ones who should decide the
merits of the educational program. They are the ones who are in a position to
know.

The teacher's argument depends on a decision principle that can be expressed roughly as follows: *Any decision that, if it is to be made correctly, depends
on possessing knowledge of whether some propositions are true or false should be made
by those who possess that knowledge.* Or more simply and as Plato put it, "Those
who know should rule." Fred Cantor's teachers claim that they are entitled to
decide about the program in moral education because they are the people who
possess the knowledge required to make the decision competently.

Let us grant the plausibility of this idea. There are factual matters about
which it seems undesirable to take a vote. But does that decide the matter?
Perhaps we should also ask about the kinds of issues where voting is most
appropriate. We would suggest that voting is most appropriate when the
question to be decided is what people want. Voting can be thought of as a way
of aggregating preferences that shows maximum respect for the wants and
interests of everyone.

A central feature of the moral perspective that we have argued for in this
book is that the choices of moral agents are to be respected because they are
the choices of moral agents. One conclusion we derived from this was that free
people have a right to their own conception of their good. No one has a right
to decide what we should value. At the same time, we cannot all have all of
what we want. Moreover, collective decisions must be made about some
things, and these decisions will affect the ability of people to succeed in
realizing their chosen values.

If this is true, then what seems required is a decision-making process that respects the freely chosen values of individuals to the maximum extent possible. Democracy is such a decision-making process. The two basic features of democracy with which we began this discussion serve these ends. That is, by adopting a decision-making process that fairly considers the wants of each individual and that gives each individual a fair chance to affect decisions, we exhibit respect for the freely chosen values of individuals.

If we see democracy as a way of aggregating preferences, we do not run into the absurdity of attempting to determine truth by vote. For in deciding what people collectively want, we are not attempting to decide the truth of any proposition. Instead, we are attempting to make a decision that shows the maximum possible respect for the freely chosen values of all.

This view suggests a kind of division of labor between democratic decision making and decision making by experts. The general idea of this division of labor is that when decisions turn primarily on determining what people collectively want, decisions should be made democratically, but when decisions turn primarily on matters of fact that require some expertise, they should be made by experts. This view can be captured by the suggestion that policy decisions should be made democratically, but should be implemented by experts.

It is obvious, however, that this division of labor is too simple. Policies are not simply statements of preferences. Often, for example, the rational selection of a policy depends on a great deal of factual knowledge. Nevertheless, we believe that the division of labor we have suggested between democratic decision making and expertise has much to commend it. In a representative democracy, the primary function of the legislature (school boards are legislative bodies) is to consider the interests of the individuals it represents and integrate them in a way that gives fullest expression to the diversity of interests involved. Thus, the primary determinant of a democratic decision is the interests of the citizens. Legislative bodies become undemocratic when their decisions are not made in the interests of their citizens.

Government employees (including teachers) are obligated to implement policy. This does not mean that employees may not exercise judgment or that they must somehow be mere mindless and docile executors of the decisions of legislative bodies. It does mean, however, that such choices as they make must be subservient to legislated policy. What makes the behavior of government employees undemocratic is the substitution of their own purposes and goals (including their views as to what is good for citizens) for those that have been democratically chosen. In a democracy, expertise should be subservient to democratically determined goals.

The implication of this for our case is to weaken the argument that can be made for the teachers. In voting down the program of moral education, the board has expressed the will of the citizens concerning the goals the educational system of the district should serve. The teachers' opposition to the board's decision is not merely based on some difference about how agreed-upon goals are to be achieved. Instead, it is a disagreement about what goals are to be served. The teachers have placed their views about educational policy above the democratically chosen goals of the district. To do this, in effect, is to claim that experts may determine what is good for others. It may or may not be the case that teachers are experts in pedagogy and should have the dominant voice in deciding how educational goals should be accomplished. But Fred Cantor's teachers have put themselves in the position of deciding the educational good of the community for the community. The view of democracy we have sketched suggests no grounds for their doing so.

It is important to be clear that this argument concerns sovereignty, not expert input or participation. That is, we are claiming that our arguments for democratic control of education locate ultimate responsibility for and authority over education in the democratically elected board. They do not show that boards of education should not solicit input into policy questions from teachers and administrators. Clearly teachers and administrators do know things about education and do have a sense of what constitutes a sound education. Their participation in the board's deliberations about policy is valuable and should be routinely sought. Democracy does not prevent legislative bodies from consulting with or taking the advice of knowledgeable people. Nor does it preclude substantial delegation of decision-making responsibility to teachers in their areas of expertise. But we believe that it does prevent the transmission of their sovereignty as representatives of the community. Democratic sovereignty includes the right to ignore good advice. Legislative bodies have the right to be wrong.

The last question we promised to raise is the justification of democracy. It is one we need not long address, because we have already answered it in dealing with the other issues. Democracy is justified because it shows respect for persons. The two rules of democratic decision making do this in that they require respect for the wants and interests of all and that they grant everyone a fair chance to influence decisions. Democracy thus respects both the freely chosen values of all and the right of each to decide for him- or herself. It treats each person as an end, not a means to the ends of others.

This justification is obviously a nonconsequentialist one. There are, of course, many consequentialist arguments for democracy. It is often claimed, for example, that democratic decision making, by requiring full discussion of issues, ultimately produces the best decisions or that democracy is the only form of decision making that can consistently produce peaceful resolution of disagreements. We have no reason here to reject such consequentialist arguments. If true, they are a bonus. Again, however, we claim that they are not morally basic. The chief moral virtue of democracy is its treatment of each person as a free moral agent whose decisions and values should be respected. Good consequences may flow from that, but they are not the basic justification for democratic decision making; respect for persons is.

ANALYSIS: OBJECTIVE MORAL REASONING

The incomplete part of our agenda is to ask if we have made a case that objective moral reasoning is possible. Certainly we have been able to provide reasons for all sorts of things. There seems to be some argument for each side of every case, even though we have tried to show that nonconsequentialism is a better basis for ethics than consequentialism. Are such issues ever decidable? If so, how?

It would be a mistake to conclude from the ambiguous character of the cases we analyzed and the others included in this book that moral deliberations can never be rationally concluded. In simpler cases, in our everyday lives as educators, we do reach reasonable and justifiable moral decisions about such things as plagiarism, theft, and honesty, for example. Our cases in this book have been constructed to be difficult and ambiguous. It is their ambiguity that makes them interesting and useful as a teaching tool. We are not even sure that each of our cases could be rationally and objectively decided in some conclusive way.

This is not decisive, however. We should be careful not to conclude too much from cases of moral ambiguity or moral disagreement. It is commonly argued that ethics is relative to culture because human beings disagree about moral questions and different societies have different moral points of view. The conclusion does not follow from the premises. It simply does not follow that, if two people or two cultures disagree, no one is right. Different cultures have different views of medicine as well. However, we need not conclude that if some people believe that disease is caused by evil spirits, the germ theory of disease is incorrect. Nor need we conclude that the truth about medicine is relative to culture. It makes a good deal more sense to conclude that one of the views is incorrect.

Likewise, it does not follow from the fact that something is unknown that it is unknowable. If we do not currently know the answer to an ethical question, it does not follow that we may not be able to discover the answer by careful reflection and inquiry or that someone else at some later time may not solve the problem. If ethics is an area of human inquiry in which we search for the best principles that we can find to regulate human conduct, then we should expect that there will be ethical discoveries. Slavery was once morally controversial. Have not human beings "discovered" it to be wrong?

Finally, it is a mistake to expect a degree of precision from an inquiry that it is incapable of providing. In this century, even mathematics has been embarrassed by the discovery that there are mathematical questions that can be shown to be unanswerable. It does not follow that mathematical reasoning lacks objectivity or that mathematical truth is relative to culture. Likewise, it does not follow from the fact that some ethical questions are difficult or even undecidable that ethical reasoning has no point or that no ethical questions can be decided. In some cases, if nothing else, we make significant progress if we can become clearer about the nature of the difficulty itself. Sometimes, too, we can resolve a matter, at least for ourselves, by discovering that it connects with our basic principles in a certain way. If the process of moral deliberation is not always decisive or clear, or completely objective, it is also rarely fruitless. Moral reasoning and debate always gets us somewhere, and as moral agents we are obligated to participate in it.

If moral ambiguity and disagreement do not force us to conclude that ethical argument has no point, neither do they show us that, or how, legitimate moral argument is possible. Here we owe the reader at least a brief account of our view of moral methodology. Our position can be easily sketched, but not quite so easily defended. The central ideas are these: Moral decisions regarding choice and action require moral sensitivity, rationality, and the development of moral theory for which the initial evidence is our moral intuitions. Moral intuitions—that is, our intuitive sense of what is right and wrong—are important data for moral reasoning and the construction of moral theory.

Not every moral intuition is equally useful, however. We should begin with those that seem most compelling and least controversial. Constructing a moral theory, then, proceeds through attempts to formulate principles that account for these moral intuitions. It is not our intuitions themselves that are inconclusive. We must be able to describe the underlying moral concepts that generate our sense of right and wrong, to discover the implicit rules that cause us to feel the way we do. It is not just taking whatever pops into our hearts and heads as right or wrong; it is looking for the bases of our intuitions, describing and analyzing them, and then testing them to the best of our ability. In this way we move from simple intuition to a more sophisticated, objective, rational, and reflective approach to ethics.

In this respect, constructing a moral theory is much like attempting to describe the rules governing our sense of grammar. We have intuitions about how to use language correctly and meaningfully without necessarily being able to formulate the rules of our language. This sense of what is meaningful or correct to say provides the data against which to test sets of rules postulated to explain our sense of grammar. In fact, that is how grammarians do grammar. They will ask themselves such questions as "Why does 'all good boys eat cake' make sense and 'cake boys good eat all' not make sense?" Likewise, we must make clear and explicit the rules and principles that underlie our moral intuitions.

The analogy goes even deeper. Sometimes a deep understanding of the principles of language can lead us to revise our initial opinion about what is meaningful or correct. Understanding the principle can make clear and comprehensible an expression that seemed obscure or ambiguous, or it can lead us to see the awkwardness or obscurity of something that had appeared clear and simple. Likewise, a moral theory can change or overrule our intuitions about moral phenomena. Once we see more clearly what is assumed by our moral intuitions, we may wish to change our minds. Thus there is an interaction between moral theory and moral intuition in rational ethical reflection, each influencing the other. The trick is to achieve some point of reflective equilibrium between our moral sense and our moral theory. By reflective equilibrium we mean reaching a point in our deliberations where we feel that our moral intuitions and the moral theory that accounts for them are satisfactorily consistent and where the decisions we reach and actions we take can be objectively justified by our moral theory. Of course, as with scientific theory, new facts, events, and hypotheses can force us to reconsider and reformulate our moral theory and to alter our decisions and actions.

Moral theories must meet the standards common to judging theories of all sorts. They must explain the data appropriate to them. They must be consistent. Elegance, parsimony, and symmetry are nice, too, when they can be had. Moral theories must also be sensitive to knowledge in other domains. Factual matters and the theories of other disciplines are important to ethical theory, not only because they are important in knowing how moral abstractions are applied to concrete cases, but also because they can suggest new problems to be solved or alter the concepts by means of which ethical theories are articulated. Freud's discovery of the unconscious raised difficult questions about the notion of autonomy and posed new moral issues about psychological manipulations. The advances of physics and biology drove purposes from nature and required people to rethink the way in which values and purposes exist. These are things that any comprehensive moral theory must confront.

Having a comprehensive and well thought out moral theory is not enough. As feeling human beings we also need to be sensitive to the moral domain and draw upon our shared ability to empathize with and care about other persons. Our moral intuitions are rooted in our ability to feel and empathize as well as in our ability to think. We need emotion as well as reason to be moved to act morally and to care about rational moral arguments and their outcomes. Feelings interact with moral reasoning in several important ways. First, feelings help us to put ourselves in the place of others, to identify with them, to know what hurts and what helps. It will do little good to be committed to respecting the value and dignity of other persons if we cannot experience life from their point of view. How else shall we know how to respect them? How else shall we discover what counts as affirming their dignity?

Second, feelings provide motivation for right conduct. If one could build a computer capable of engaging in moral reasoning, its chief defect would probably be that it would not care about being moral. Knowing what is right and wanting to do it are different things. Our ability to empathize, to experience the wrong done to others as our hurt and the good done to others as our joy, is a large part of our desire to do right. Immanuel Kant, who had many wise things to say about ethics, said nothing wiser than that the only really good thing is a good will.

How, then, do we settle ethical arguments? We proceed first by trying to discover the moral principles that underlie our differing senses of right and wrong. When we see what it is that our moral intuitions assume, perhaps some of us will change our minds. If not, then we must test our conflicting moral principles by seeing what else follows from them. If we find that some proposed principle leads to an abhorrent or implausible result in certain cases, that is a reason to abandon it. Perhaps some will change their minds when they see what else they must agree to if they are to hold consistently to their current positions.

Where does our sense of right and wrong come from? This question would seem to bear on how possible it is to establish an objective, reflective equilibrium about ethical issues. Some philosophers have argued that our sense of morality is innate. Theologians may add that it is God-given. Others have suggested that moral intuitions are a kind of seeing. There are moral facts that we can see with our mind's eye, just as we see colors with our physical eye. Still others assume that we learn our moral principles, just as we learn our native language, from our culture. Does it matter? One might argue that if moral concepts are innate or God-given or involve seeing moral facts that have objective existence, then this certifies the objectivity of moral thought. Moral questions, like questions about the physical world, have answers. These answers are, somehow, grounded in the nature of reality. On the other hand, if we acquire those principles that generate our moral intuitions from our culture, this means that, fundamentally, relativism is still true. The best that moral reasoning could be expected to do in that case would be to produce a higher level of agreement among those who already agree about basic assumptions.

We cannot here resolve the issue of where our sense of right and wrong comes from. Instead, we want to suggest that the question of where our moral intuitions come from is not that decisive for the objectivity of moral reasoning. Seeing it as decisive rests on inflated demands for what will be permitted to count as objective knowledge and on an excessive pessimism about human commonalities. If we demand certainty of moral knowledge or if we demand that all legitimate knowledge somehow must be certain and beyond challenge and change in the light of new evidence, we may find knowledge difficult to come by—and not only about ethics. But if we insist only on establishing a provisional reflective equilibrium based on our best reasoned judgment at the time, we will have set a standard for objectivity that can often be met and will serve us well in our lives. What is the point of setting our standards for objective knowledge in a way that makes a fundamental and necessary human activity, that of reflecting on what we ought to do, appear impossible?

Moreover, even if our ethical intuitions are acquired from our society, it does not follow that reflective equilibrium among members of different societies is impossible. To the degree that societies are different, we may expect the search for reflective moral equilibrium to be difficult. To assume that it is impossible is to neglect the extent to which all societies are composed of people with a common biology, common fundamental needs and feelings, a common physical environment, and common aspirations. It is also to neglect the extent to which we live on a planet whose people are increasingly united by a common science and by common global problems. The commonalities are basic to our view of the source of the moral intuitions of human beings. We are not all so alike that reflective equilibrium about moral matters is likely to be easy. We are not all so different that it must be impossible. Some of us would even argue that we see writ large in human history a positive development toward a more humane and more broadly shared ethical point of view. There are, then, some good reasons to keep open the possibility of humanly arrived at ethical knowledge. We can be objective and reasonable even if we cannot be certain, and we can be tolerant and open to other points of view without being relativists.

Nevertheless, there is a common but misguided incentive for the prevalent modern belief in moral relativism. It is the human desire to be free, to be unencumbered by duties and obligations. If we may misparaphrase Dostoevsky, people seem to believe that if relativism is true, then everything is permitted. Each of us may do as we choose, and no one can tell us that we are wrong or that we must do something else. The idea is often captured in the suggestion that people who argue that something is genuinely right or wrong are, in reality, attempting to impose their views on others.

This response is both confused and problematic. It is confused in that it identifies compulsion with persuasion. When one person attempts to give reasons to another person, that act is not an attempt at coercion. Indeed, persuasion is a form of influence that recognizes individuals as free moral agents with rational minds and human feelings. To attempt to persuade someone is to assume that the choice is theirs and that as responsible moral agents they would wish to make it on the basis of the best reasons available. To give people reasons is to confirm their status as free individuals who have the right to choose for themselves.

Seeing persuasion as a kind of coercion ultimately rests on a failure to understand the ultimate moral basis of freedom. We are not free because we have no objective duties. Nothing about freedom follows from moral relativism, because nothing at all concerning ethical matters can follow from relativism. We are free because we are moral agents with the duty to decide for ourselves and because it is morally offensive to interfere arbitrarily with the liberty of a person who has the moral duty to make responsible choices.

It is often claimed that what sets human beings off from other living creatures is their ability to reason. From our point of view, we humans also share the distinctive capacity to have and choose to have obligations. To ask what moral obligations we should accept is to presume that we are free to choose and that good reasons can be given for some choices and against others. And the giving of reasons presumes that reasons provide objective grounds for reaching potential agreements and progressive states of reflective equilibrium and moral growth.

Relativism is problematic in that, if taken seriously, it can lead us to withhold resources that are important for moral growth. People do not learn to make responsible choices by being told that it does not matter what they decide, since one choice is as valid as another. They learn to make responsible choices by learning to appraise arguments and consider evidence relevant to what they have to decide. Such things are best learned by participating in a milieu in which ethical matters are seriously considered and debated. Moral relativism undermines the moral education appropriate to a free people.

Finally, we believe that moral relativism undermines the administrator's sense of his or her task. We see education as a profoundly moral enterprise. Its purpose is to develop educated citizens who can function as free people in a free and self-governing society. The moral commitments we have examined in this book — intellectual and personal liberty, equality, due process, and democracy — are more than simply concepts that provide handy vehicles for learning to think about ethical problems. They are more than concepts that are important to thinking about doing the work of an administrator. They are concepts that are central to our vision of ourselves as a free people. Thus they should be central to our view of education in a free society.

The administrator who is an ethical relativist cannot share in this vision. Such a person sees freedom, equality, and democracy as morally arbitrary, as things that some people happen to value, but that have no compelling objective justification. Such a view of these basic moral principles is hardly likely to inspire a reasoned commitment to them that guides daily decision making. The administrator who is an ethical relativist must either be uncommitted to the underlying principles of our society or irrationally committed to them. Neither seems especially desirable.

Finally, the administrator who believes in ethical relativism is likely to see administration as essentially a technical enterprise. If administrative behavior is to be based on objective knowledge, that knowledge can only be factual knowledge of how to accomplish given objectives. Values should not enter the picture. The relativistic administrator, thus, will concern himself or herself with how most efficiently to accomplish pre-identified goals. Such individuals quickly become manipulators of other human beings, unconcerned about the ethics of school administration and focused only on completing the tasks at hand. Such individuals also renounce responsibility for judging the educational and moral worth of the objectives and policies they are given by others. Like the administrators and guards of concentration camps, they only follow orders. Theirs is not to reason why. There is no point to moral reasoning.

CONCLUSION

The question of the possibility of objective moral reasoning is crucial both for our view of education and our view of administration. A belief in the possibility of moral reasoning permits a view of education that is itself moral in nature. It provides the grounds for administrators to pursue, with their staff and students, those moral commitments that define us as a free people in a free and democratic society. Ethical relativism, in contrast, leaves the administrator to pursue values that cannot be objectively chosen and thus, if operative at all, must be arbitrarily imposed. Moreover, relativism defines the administrative role as technical and manipulative. It treats people as means, not as ends, and views respect for persons as just one among many arbitrary value judgments. To us the choice is obvious. Moral relativism is a belief that no responsible and rational administrator can follow in practice.

ADDITIONAL CASES

Democracy in Action

"Who? Who the hell won?" Don Patterson, superintendent of Mayville public schools exploded. "Who are those people? They weren't even running! How could they have been elected to the school board?"

Patterson was sitting at the breakfast table with his wife and listening to the local news on the radio. He had turned it on to hear the results of yesterday's school board election. Actually, he had turned it on to hear what the turnout had been, not to find out who had won. The winners, he had thought, were a foregone conclusion. Three seats on Mayville's board of education had to be filled. The three persons who held those seats had sought reelection. They were running unopposed. Under those conditions, how could they not win?

Voter turnout, on the other hand, was very problematic. Like residents in most school districts in the United States, relatively few of Mayville's citizens bothered to vote in school board elections. Ordinarily, about 15% of those eligible actually cast ballots (a figure quite comparable to the national average). In the previous two elections, however, this percentage had declined even further; last year fewer than 8% of the town's citizens had gone to the polls.

These low turnouts were a matter of concern to Patterson. He had hoped that voters would begin to evidence a greater interest in their schools than they had in the recent past. Realistically, though, he knew there was little hope that this election would generate much interest. After all, there was no real choice to be made. Why go to the polls when the outcome was preordained? Apparently most of the good burghers of Mayville felt the same way; less than 4% of the citizens had voted in yesterday's election, according to the reporter.

Someone had obviously taken an interest in the election, however. The three incumbents had all been defeated by seemingly unknown, phantom candidates. Their defeat disturbed the superintendent considerably. The three incumbents had been good board members. They worked at their task, and they were not mouthpieces for any special interest group in the community. For example, they had stood firm during the last round of contract negotiations against union attempts to gain significant new controls over district policy making.

Patterson gave his full attention to the newscaster. She seemed as perplexed by the election as he. The three winners were Mary Rellihan, John Jacobson, and Henry Martin, all of whom were obviously as unknown to the reporter as they were to the superintendent. The three had been elected as write-in candidates, defeating the three incumbents by comfortable margins. The station was in the process of contacting the winners to obtain interviews and would have the full story in a later broadcast, the newscaster concluded.

"How could write-ins defeat people whose names are on the ballot?" Patterson asked his wife as he switched off the radio. "They'd have to mount a public campaign to get people to vote for them, and there hasn't been any such campaign. These people are completely unknown."

"Well, I don't know about two of them, but isn't Jacobson the fellow who helped the Mayville Teachers' Association write those position papers a few years back?" Patterson's wife asked.

The superintendent reflected a moment. "You know, I think you're right," he said. He leaned back in his chair and thought a few seconds longer. "In fact, now that you mention it, I'll bet that the MTA has had something to do with this. I'm going to get hold of Cleaver when I get to the office and find out."

An hour later Bill Cleaver, the president of the MTA, stood smiling at Patterson. "I had a hunch you'd want to talk to me this morning, Don," he said. "You've probably got a few questions about yesterday's election results."

In the next hour, Patterson got a lesson in practical politics from the union president, who was obviously feeling rather pleased with himself and his association.

Cleaver began by saying that the MTA had been very unhappy with the three incumbent board members who were running for reelection. Throughout their terms they had taken positions that the MTA considered "anti-teacher." Further, they were articulate and persuasive. They always managed to convince at least one other person on the seven-member board of the correctness of their views. Hence the three had succeeded in getting a significant number of policy changes enacted that tilted the balance of power toward the board and away from the teachers. That the MTA should be unhappy with them hardly surprised Patterson. The union's method of handling its unhappiness was a surprise, however.

It seemed that several months ago the MTA executive council had made a deliberate decision not to publicly back a slate of candidates in opposition to the three incumbents. "This town's so anti-union that if the MTA backed Mother Teresa for the board, she'd lose," Cleaver had said. Therefore, rather than encouraging three persons to run and openly supporting them, the MTA had organized the write-in campaign. Cleaver insisted that this campaign had not been secret, however. "We simply didn't publicize it," he said. "The MTA isn't under any obligation to make its decisions and actions public."

The union had correctly foreseen that voter turnout would be low, especially if the three incumbents were thought to be running unopposed. Accordingly, its executive council had quietly sought out three persons in the community who were sympathetic to the MTA's position on various issues and who would agree to run as unannounced write-in candidates. Then, just a week prior to the election, the executive council had called a closed meeting of the entire MTA membership. It had presented its three candidates and explained its election strategy. Basically, it urged members to write in the names of the three and to get a few supportive family members and friends to do likewise. "We explained," Cleaver said, "that if each MTA member got only four other persons to write in our candidates' names, they would almost certainly win, as long as the voter turnout stayed below 5%. So," he concluded, "we told them not to 'get out the vote' but to get out four certain write-in voters. And we told them to keep a very low profile in doing so. It worked beautifully."

"A new era in teacher-board relations is about to begin," Cleaver concluded. "Instead of being at each other's throats, the MTA and the Mayville Board of Education can finally establish a cooperative and harmonious relationship. Education in this town is bound to improve." He paused and then laughed. "Of course, your job will probably be a little tougher, Don, now that the board's not in your pocket. But that's okay. That's why you superintendents get those fat salaries."

Some Questions

1. Under "Concept: Democracy" earlier in this chapter, we said that a decision has been made democratically if two conditions are met. Has anything undemocratic happened in Mayville? If so, what?
2. The facts mentioned in the case regarding the low turnouts in school board elections in this country are correct. Why should low turnouts be characteristic of these elections? What does this say about "local control"?
3. Do low turnouts necessarily mean that many people's views are not represented on the school board? Does that mean that they do not have a fair influence on a decision?
4. What, if anything, should Patterson do regarding his three new board members? Should he say or do anything about the MTA's election strategy? If so, what?

Are Schools More Important than Sewers?

Editor,
Urbanville *Star Tribune*
Urbanville, New York 14850

Dear Sir:

We, the teachers of the Urbanville Teachers' Association, must protest the recent action of the school board that froze teacher hiring for next year. We recognize that the board has had little choice in the matter, given the recent unconscionable decision of the Urbanville City Council. Nevertheless, as professional educators responsible to the children of this city, we cannot let the board's action go unchallenged.

It is important that readers of the *Star Tribune* understand exactly what is at issue. The Urbanville School District is a fiscally dependent one. That means that the school board must submit its budget to the city council for approval, along with submissions from all other departments of city government, for example, Parks and Recreation, Human Services, Sanitation, and Streets and Sewers. On September 15 of last year the city council cut almost $2 million from the district's original submission. After negotiation, the district was able to get some of this money restored, but next year's budget is still almost $1.5 million lower than this year. The ostensible reason for this draconian cut was the disrepair of the city's sewers. The city council claimed that Urbanville's sewers are in such poor condition that money must be diverted from other city services to repair and replace them because taxes could not be raised any further. In effect, the council has claimed that sewers are more important than schools.

In response to this cut in its budget, the school board has had to find a way to reduce the services it offers to the children of Urbanville. It has chosen to freeze staff hiring for next year. Since 45 teachers are expected to retire or otherwise leave the system in June, the pupils of those teachers will have to be absorbed into the classes of those of us who remain. We estimate that the average class size in the district will increase by nearly five pupils.

We doubt that either the school board or the public fully understands the impact of this change. Already our classes are too large, and it is extremely difficult to provide the individual attention pupils need. Next year, with even larger classes, it will be impossible. As just one example of the cut's effects, careful grading of all assignments will become a hopeless task.

In order to demonstrate to the public the consequences of the board's decision, the members of the teachers' association have voted to take a drastic action. Beginning next week, we will cease giving assignments that require a large amount of out-of-school time to grade. For example, weekly essays will no longer be assigned in ninth-grade English, and senior themes will not be required. Next year, with even larger classes than we currently have, such assignments will not be feasible. We teachers are willing to tighten our belts and contribute our share to the solution of the city's fiscal crisis. We are unwilling to pay for sewer repairs with time taken from our own families.

We deeply regret taking this action. However, we have been given no choice. We think that the Board's decision is unjustified. We believe that the school board, instead of meekly submitting to the ill-considered actions of the city council, has the duty to resist these cuts; we demand that the children of Urbanville receive the education they deserve. Education is more important than sewers!

Respectfully,

Allan A. Grimshaw
President, UTA

Some Questions

1. Well, is that true? Is education more important than sewers? How do you know? How are such questions decided in a democracy?
2. What role do experts have in such decisions? Specifically, what is the proper

role of teachers in deciding the relative importance of education compared to other governmental services?

3. We have said that government policies almost always contain factual as well as valuational premises. Thus elected representatives can democratically and collectively make a mistake. What are professional educators to do when a community democratically arrives at a mistaken judgment about what is educationally worthwhile?

4. Urbanville's teachers are set to engage in a kind of job action often called a "slowdown," a collective action occupying a middle ground between doing nothing and striking. Are such actions appropriate for professional employees?

5. Fiscal dependency is relatively uncommon among U.S. school districts. (Most school boards adopt a budget and levy whatever taxes that budget requires.) Make a case for fiscal dependency as a mode for funding schools. That is, argue that city councils, not school boards, should set school budgets.

Educational Auditors

Tom Summerset, the district's superintendent, had been entirely unprepared for the final recommendation in Dr. Williamson's report. Obviously he had not been very persuasive when it came up for board discussion, either. The board had adopted Williamson's idea that the district establish an Office of Educational Audit.

Williamson was a professor of educational administration at Northeast State University. He had been hired by the Midville board of education as a consultant to study the district's administrative organization and to make recommendations regarding its restructuring. Most of his recommendations had been innocuous enough. They concerned the usual kinds of things: curriculum committees, decreased centralization, and a few changes in role relationships. Summerset thought all of these were sensible. It was the last recommendation that was a bombshell.

In his report to the board, Williamson had noted that a critical problem in all organizations is the quality of upward communication. Upward communication is the principal method by which people at the top of an organization, especially those serving on a governing board, learn how well the organization is functioning and what policy changes are necessary. Unless the governing board has accurate information about the success of the organization in meeting board objectives, it cannot govern in a rational manner. When that happens in the case of school districts, he claimed, the people no longer control their schools through their elected representatives. Instead, and to the degree that the organization is governed at all, it is controlled by the professional educators.

Williamson claimed that his study had found that this was a particularly severe problem in Midville. The board of education was even more ignorant of how their school system was doing than most school boards. It was entirely dependent on whatever information trickled upward to it from the lowest levels of the system, or whatever information it could gain from (usually disgruntled) citizens who happened to call board members and complain about something.

Basically, Williamson had said that the upward flow of accurate information was inhibited because everyone—teachers, principals, and the superintendent—was less likely to report their difficulties and deficiencies to their superiors than they were to report their achievements. Thus teachers were more likely to tell their principals about their successes than their failures; principals would do the same when reporting to the superintendent; and the superintendent did the same when reporting to the board of education. The net result of all of these constrictions in the upward flow of unfavorable information was that boards of education always thought things were going better in their districts than they in fact were. This, he said, was particularly true of Midville.

Williamson was careful to stress that the problem was not that Midville's educators deliberately lied to their superiors. Indeed, he praised the quality of the district's professional staff. Rather, the difficulty arose because lines of organizational communication were also lines of organizational authority. Thus the classic bureaucratic pattern required everyone to voluntarily report their failures and difficulties to precisely that person who was responsible for evaluating their performance. Such an expectation was patently unrealistic for ordinary mortals. It was only human for people to put the best face on their work when discussing it with their superiors. Hence, Williamson concluded, everyone tended to downplay problems and emphasize successes, with predictable consequences for the board of education's knowledge about the system's actual performance and its ability to govern the district rationally for the benefit of Mayville's citizens.

Williamson's solution to this organizational problem was as simple in its conception as it was revolutionary in its implications. He proposed that the Midville Board of Education establish an Office of Educational Audit. Basically, this office would involve a trained educational evaluator who would be responsible for providing the board with accurate information on any topic of the board's choosing. Thus, for example, if the board had a decision to make about reading programs, it might pose a series of questions about those programs to the auditor. The auditor would then collect the information the board wanted and prepare it for its use in making a decision. Regular administrators would be substantially freed from preparing evaluation reports for the board of education.

What was revolutionary about this suggestion was the place of the Office of Educational Auditor in Midville's organizational pyramid. Williamson recommended that the auditor report directly to the board. Auditors would receive their orders from the board and report their findings to the board. Further, they would have full access to any classroom or office in the district, and they would be free to gather whatever information they needed to answer the questions posed by the board. In effect, the office was at the highest level of the school system's hierarchy and simultaneously had direct access to the lowest level of the hierarchy. It effectively cut out all of the middle layers that restricted the upward flow of negative information, giving the board direct access to events at the working level of the school district.

Finally, the auditor's reports to the board would be untainted by the inevitable bias created by the usual organizational confounding of lines of authority with lines of communication. This was because the auditor would be responsible only for the quality of the information provided to the board, not for the success or failure of any of the district's educational programs. If the auditor brought the board bad news about a program, that would not reflect on his or her job performance. Thus, the auditor could be an unbiased observer for the board (and hence the public), with no reason to see things in either a favorable or unfavorable light.

Summerset found everything about Williamson's idea distasteful. The consultant had stressed that the school board was charged with making educational policy decisions on behalf of the community. In order to do that, the board needed high-quality information. However, Summerset recognized that the auditor might very well provide information that conflicted with the information that he, the superintendent, provided. What was he supposed to do in that case? Whom would the board believe? Further, Summerset considered the whole scheme an unsubtle slap at his ability. It suggested that he, as superintendent, was unable to provide accurate information to his board. He resented the fact that the auditor, a member of the district's staff, would not be hired by him, would not be responsible to him, and could not be fired by him. Most of all, the whole idea would obviously result in a very substantial shift in power from the professional staff to the lay board of education.

Summerset reflected ruefully to himself: He should have known better than to let the board hire Williamson. What the hell do ivory tower academics—especially professors of educational administration—know about running a school district?

Some Questions

1. How would the auditor proposal affect the balance of power among the board, the superintendent, and the teachers?
2. Would the presence of an auditor make the operations of the Mayville district more or less democratic?

3. Might the auditor have a negative effect on the morale of Mayville's teachers and administrators? If so, is this a reason for not having one?
4. Would the creation of such a system suggest that teachers or administrators are not professionals? If so, is this a reason for not doing it?
5. Might the creation of such a system violate anyone's rights of due process or privacy?
6. Might an increase in teacher autonomy make a school district less democratic, but more effective? If so, which should we prefer and why?

CHAPTER 7

Supplemental Cases

CASE #1: A MATTER OF HONESTY

Mr. Blain enjoyed looking through travel guides. He especially liked looking through guides to warm and sunny spots when the temperature at home was below zero and the snow was piled up to his office windows. Northern Minnesota had many things to commend it as a place to live and work. In Mr. Blain's opinion, however, February wasn't one of them.

Fortunately, the Board of Education of Allen Federated Schools provided its superintendent with a generous allowance for professional improvement. This allowance could be used to pay for travel to professional meetings. Generally it was enough to cover airfare to remote and warm spots such as Florida, Arizona, and southern California. It would even stretch to include a week in a good hotel and some first-rate dinners.

The trick was to find a good professional meeting in the right place at the right time. Fortunately, those folk who organized conferences for superintendents were attentive to the pleasant effects of warmth and available sunshine on conference attendance. In the winter there was always something plausible going on down South.

Of course, Mr. Blain had to admit that once or twice he had gone to conferences that were of little interest to him. There was the trip to the Urban Education Society meetings last year. His district was hardly urban. Indeed, the local deer population outnumbered the student population. And then there was the conference on artificial intelligence five years back. He had not understood a word of the one session he had attended. Still, there was something to be said for attending a conference that was of minimal interest to him. It interfered less with his recreation.

Not that Mr. Blain was entirely inattentive to his superintendently duties while he was away. He generally took along some work, and he went to conference sessions when they seemed to deal with something of potential value for his district. Indeed, Mr. Blain felt that the district got its money's worth. He often learned something of use, and when he did not he came back

115

warm and rested and was able to devote more time and effort to the welfare of his school system. It was a fair trade.

Nor was the arrangement likely to cause trouble. The board of education always approved his trips even though their recreational potential was evident. He made no attempt to hide his tan on return. The arrangement had evolved into a kind of fringe benefit. It was good for him, did not hurt his district, and no one raised objections. Why shouldn't he use his professional development money for a midwinter vacation?

Some Questions

1. Do you believe that Mr. Blain is acting dishonestly or unethically? Why or why not?
2. Does the fact that the board of education has tacitly accepted his midwinter vacation justify it? If they simply granted him a paid midwinter vacation as a fringe benefit would that justify it?
3. Suppose it really is true that Mr. Blain is a more effective superintendent because of his midwinter vacation. Does that justify it?

CASE #2: A MATTER OF INTEGRITY

Her orders were clear. She had done her best to change the decision, but the board would not agree. She was required to implement it. But she could not. She was deeply convinced not only that it was a mistake, but that it was wrong.

Sandra Jones had been the principal of the New Hope alternative middle school for about 15 years. During that time she had forged a successful alternative school that served the children electing to attend it very well. The children who attended it came from a variety of backgrounds and possessed an enormous range of abilities. They had one thing in common. They did not function well in the usual classroom. Some of the students were conventional behavior problems. They were not academically talented and had rebelled against schools that seemed persistently interested in demonstrating their inferiority to others. Some of her students were, however, enormously talented. But they had difficulty seeing why they should learn what someone else had picked for them instead of pursuing their own interests. Mrs. Jones's students were the academically alienated.

She ran a school with few rules, many of which students worked out for themselves. Students' programs were highly individualized. The only real requirement was that students spend their time profitably. Persistent goofing-off was not long tolerated. Older or more gifted students were used to teach younger or less gifted ones. The teachers provided much individual instruction and even more individual counseling.

Sandra Jones considered her school a great success. She had built a school community. Old students helped initiate new students into the life of the school. Many students were reclaimed, going on to become good citizens and productive people. The achievement scores for her students were only slightly below the district average. Given the students she worked with, some of whom simply filled out standardized tests randomly to express their distaste for testing, she thought this to be remarkable.

Unhappily, the board of education and the new superintendent were not similarly impressed. What they were impressed by was the demand for excellence which meant to them higher expectations, more discipline, more required courses and more testing. They had not been pleased with what they saw at New Hope. Its program was not consistent with their concept of excellence.

Last year, the board had decided to study New Hope. They had appointed a subcommittee headed by the new superintendent. The subcommittee had recently reported and made its recommendations. The report bemoaned the lack of excellence at New Hope. While they recommended that it continue to exist, that it function as the alternative school for the district, and that Sandra Jones continue to be its principal, they also recommended that New Hope conform to the curriculum and the discipline practices followed elsewhere in the district. Despite her vigorous protests, the board adopted the recommendations. The new superintendent assured the board that they would be strictly followed.

Sandra knew that these new policies would destroy the program she had carefully constructed. She believed that it would destroy many of New Hope's students, and some of its teachers as well. She simply could not implement the board's recommendations.

She had intended to resign. She could not follow board policy with a clear conscience. When she had expressed her intent to some of her teachers, however, they suggested another alternative. They suggested that she seek to subvert board policy. One teacher suggested, "Why not just tell them what they want to hear and do what you want?" Within a few days she had heard essentially the same message from a number of teachers and students.

She thought that this might just be possible. There was a great deal of ambiguity in the language of the recommendations. Moreover, neither the board nor the superintendent had shown much inclination to come to New Hope for inspection trips. She was their main source of information. It would be possible to make a few cosmetic changes and continue with business as usual. At least she could give it a try.

The trouble was that this strategy felt wrong. She would be being devious and would be subverting board policy. She felt uncomfortable about both of those. On the other hand, her school had become crucial to the lives of many of her students. Was it right to quit and abandon them to someone who would enforce board policy with enthusiasm? Perhaps with a bit of guile she could salvage much of her program. Should she try?

Some Questions

1. Does Sandra Jones have a moral obligation to resign her position if she believes that she cannot conscientiously implement board policy? Why might this be the case?
2. Is it wrong for her to attempt to subvert board policy if the results of doing so are genuinely beneficial for her students? Why or why not?
3. What would you advise Sandra Jones to do?

CASE #3: MERIT OR MERCY?

Teddy Clemens vaguely remembered that he had been in favor of merit pay. That was before he had had to administer it. As principal of Red Bluff Elementary School, it had fallen to him to pick a few teachers to receive special merit raises this year. Moreover, this year the board had really gotten into the idea of merit pay. The merit bonuses were large enough to be worth having.

It was less easy to decide who was meritorious. Teddy had dutifully solicited the advice of his faculty on how he should proceed. They had made it clear that it was his choice. Apparently the matter was sufficiently contentious that the teachers wished to make sure that some administrator had to take the rap. The teachers were unwilling to participate directly in the decision. He had, however, asked that they submit letters to him suggesting who might be awarded the merit bonuses.

The teachers had willingly submitted letters. He had found the results surprising and informative. The teachers were in reasonable agreement about who the genuinely excellent teachers among them were. Only one case bothered him. That was Ann Bently.

Ann was a young teacher. She had only recently gotten tenure, and the decision was close. It was the fact that she had improved consistently over her three years' probation rather than her teaching ability per se that had persuaded Teddy to recommend her. With continued improvement, she would probably become a satisfactory teacher.

But she had not been satisfactory this year. Her teaching had deteriorated significantly. Parent complaints were on the rise. Her evaluations had been poor. She had decidedly not been meritorious. Yet she was frequently mentioned by the faculty as deserving a merit raise.

Teddy thought he understood. Ann had had a disastrous year personally. Her husband had been killed in an automobile accident. He had left her with two small children, little insurance, and a large pile of unpaid bills. He knew that Ann was financially desperate. Apparently, so did everyone else. Ann talked freely about her problems. Teddy thought that was probably healthy. But she had a unique mix of charm and vulnerability that easily roused the concern and sympathy of others. She had received a good deal of mothering and fathering from the older members of his staff. Teddy thought that was commendable. His teachers were good people. They cared about each other.

But it was clear that Ann had been the beneficiary of a sympathy vote. No one really thought her to be an excellent teacher, but everyone wanted to help her out. Thus his staff was trying to suggest subtly that he give the poor kid a break. As one letter had said, "Under the circumstances she's done well, and some extra money right now would certainly help her concentrate on her teaching."

Perhaps this was the right idea. If he gave Ann the money, it might just help her concentrate more on her job. And she certainly needed it. There was much to commend the idea. But shouldn't merit raises go to those who earn them, not to those who need them?

Some Questions

1. If you were Teddy Clemens, what would you do in this case? Why?
2. Are there cases in which, as an administrator, it is more important to consider people's needs than to give them what they deserve? Can you name a few? Why, in these cases, is humane treatment more important than just treatment?

CASE #4: A CONFLICT OF INTEREST

John Tobin, the superintendent of Claymont public schools, listened with interest to Philip McDuff's speech to the other members of the board. McDuff was giving a rather impassioned speech about how poorly paid Claymont's teachers were. McDuff should know. He was married to one of them.

McDuff was reciting a litany that had by now become familiar to almost everyone in public education. Teachers were underpaid. The teaching profession could no longer attract the best and brightest undergraduates. It could not pay them as well as science, medicine, or law. Moreover, Claymont had fallen behind other comparable districts in its pay scale. It was in danger of not being able to attract the kinds of teachers it needed. McDuff was proposing a whopping 8% increase for each of the next three years. If Tobin recalled correctly, the rate of inflation last year had been less than 2%.

It was not that Tobin was against these raises. Indeed, he was inclined to agree that his teachers were entitled to them. Moreover, high salaries made his job as an administrator easier. What made Tobin uneasy was the fact that McDuff had emerged as the leader of the "big raise" faction of the board. McDuff often allied himself with the "tax savers" rather than the spenders. Arguing for a salary increase that would require a hefty tax increase was a bit out of character. Tobin could not help but wonder if the fact that McDuff's wife would be a recipient of one of these raises had not influenced his judgment in the matter.

Of course, the fact that McDuff's wife was a teacher sometimes seemed to be an asset. McDuff often seemed to have a clearer idea of what actually went on in Claymont's classrooms than did other board members. In this case, however, it seemed to Tobin that McDuff had too much of a personal stake in the salary raises. He might at least be a bit more tactful about the matter and be quiet.

Some Questions

1. Does McDuff have a conflict of interest in this case?
2. If he does, should he avoid participating in the discussion of teacher salaries? Should he abstain from voting on them? Should he be required to abstain?
3. If McDuff's wife came up for tenure while he was on the board, how should he behave?
4. Are there other issues on which McDuff should abstain? Should teachers or their immediate families be excluded from membership on school boards?
5. Suppose you were John Tobin and that you were asked to write a policy indicating what board members should do in order to avoid such conflicts of interest. What would you suggest?

CASE #5: EXPLOITATION

"Mr. Place, I've put up with this pay for five years, but now I have a kid in college and I need the money, not just the job. You need to pay me for the work I do. I'm tired of working a full-time job for part-time wages."

Mr. Place was unsympathetic. Laura Connors had taken the job knowing quite well what it paid and what the work was. She had no right to complain now just because she thought she needed money. He felt that he was doing women like Laura Connors a service by making work available.

Laura Connors was one of a dozen women who worked in the evening division of Agamemnon High School. The evening division offered a variety of courses to the citizens of Agamemnon. Courses in photography, macramé, and oil painting were part of its fare. Laura Connors worked in the second-chance program. This program helped pregnant teens continue work toward their high school diploma.

All of the programs in the evening division were staffed in the same way. They were taught by women who worked part-time and at an hourly rate. No one was permitted to work more than 20 hours a week, since as long as they worked less than 20 hours, the school district did not have to pay them benefits. The hourly rates were low. The combined wages of two part-time teachers who worked a total of 40 hours per week were about two-thirds of the salary of one of the teachers who taught full time in the school district. Usually the teachers in the evening division had qualifications similar to the full-timers. All were college graduates, most were certified teachers, and many had master's degrees.

Even these facts were somewhat misleading so far as pay rates were concerned, for the part-time teachers generally worked more hours than they were paid. They were not actually paid for the number of hours they put in. Instead, they were paid for the number of hours at which the job was rated. The rating for the jobs generally included only the number of hours teachers were scheduled to be in the classroom, plus an hour per week of preparation time. Teachers, however, usually spent far more than one hour per week preparing for their teaching. Moreover, any time spent working with students before or after class was not compensated. It was not unusual for a teacher whose job was rated at 20 hours to actually work 30.

Mr. Place, of course, understood how Laura Connors felt. Yet he felt that his main responsibility was to provide the program. Many of its students needed the program desperately. This was especially true of the second-chance program. But the district simply could not afford these programs if it paid its part-timers at the same real wage it paid its full-time teachers. The use of low-paid part-time teachers made it possible to provide a much more extensive program than would have been otherwise possible. He felt he could not responsibly raise the pay rates and cut back the program.

Finally, he felt that wages should be determined by the market. The fact was that the Agamemnon School District had a surfeit of well-educated women. They were the wives of Agamemnon's numerous professionals. Having the research division of one the world's largest computer companies in one's district had its benefits. Most of these women were not really interested in the money. They worked because they wished for something worthwhile to do outside the home. Mr. Place could replace Laura a dozen times. If wages should be set by the market, Laura was overpaid.

He had tried to explain this to Laura. "Laura, I'm sorry I can't pay you what you're worth, but if I increased the wages of all of the people in the evening division, I'd have to cut back the program. I don't think you would want me to do that. You are a capable person. Perhaps if you really need the money, you should look for a better-paying job."

Some Questions

1. Is Laura Connors exploited?
2. How should one go about deciding what counts as fair pay? Is it important that Laura agreed to accept the job and that she could probably find a better paying job if she wished?
3. In education, part-time positions of the sort that Laura Connors occupies are predominately held by women. Is the practice of cutting costs by hiring part-timers a kind of gender discrimination?

CASE #6: BORROWED PROPERTY?

Tom Wicks had not been at Scottsdale High for more than a few months when he realized that his colleague, Fred Trevor, freely borrowed school property. But he thought that *poached* was a more accurate word.

Scottsdale was a large school, with over 3,000 students, and it had two vice-principals. Tom held one of these posts. It was his first administrative position. While his job had an impressive title, Dean of Students, actually, of course, he spent most of his time on pupil discipline. It was probably the worst job in school administration, but Tom wanted to do well at it. Someday, he hoped, he would have a school of his own.

Fred, who had been at Scottsdale for a number of years, had once been its dean of students. He had been promoted and was now its dean of instruction. That was, in Tom's judgment, an infinitely more rewarding job. Fred was responsible for curriculum, teacher evaluation, and staff development. Both Fred and Tom reported to Harry McIverson, the principal.

One Friday afternoon, shortly after Tom had arrived at Scottsdale, he and Fred happened to be walking together across the staff parking lot at the end of the school day. Fred had been trying to juggle a large box, his briefcase, and a gym bag, while getting his car keys from his pocket. Tom had offered to help by holding the box, but in the process of taking it, the carton had fallen to the ground and broken open. Inside, among other things, were several reams of paper, a couple of staplers, a tape dispenser, and several sheets of first-class postage stamps. Fred had seemed a bit embarrassed, but explained that he did much of his work at home and that he needed the supplies and equipment to do so. That seemed reasonable to Tom.

A couple of months later, when Tom was working late one evening, he glanced out his window and saw Fred on his way out of the building with a large desk lamp. Tom recognized the lamp immediately. It was one of those that had been used in the school's mechanical drawing classroom. That classroom had recently been refurbished and made into a computer room. The old equipment, including 20 or so architect's desk lamps, was currently stored in the school's basement awaiting disposition.

It was true that these lamps were now surplus. It was even possible that the district might decide to give them away to any staff members who wanted one. Nevertheless, the lamps were still district property and were worth a fair sum of money. (New, they sold for well over $100 apiece.) Tom doubted the propriety of simply appropriating one of them for home use. On the other hand, since Fred said he worked at home a lot, it was possible to argue that the district should provide him with all of the equipment he needed. Certainly a light was needed equipment; he could not be expected to work in the dark.

Last night, however, Tom had recognized that his senior colleague's borrowing exceeded the limits of propriety. Fred and his wife had thrown a cocktail party and invited Tom. A large crowd had circulated freely about the Trevors' home. During the course of the evening Tom had asked directions to a bathroom and had been routed upstairs. Walking down the hallway, he had passed an open door and noticed Chris, Fred's son, bent intently over a personal computer. Tom had stopped to say hello, and Chris had invited him in to try his hand at defeating the galactic invaders swarming over the monitor's screen. As Tom had sat down in front of the machine, he noticed the lamp angled over Chris's desk. It was a large architect's light, obviously one of those from school. Then he looked at the powerful and expensive computer in front of him. Riveted to its front panel was a tag: Property of Scottsdale Board of Education.

Some Questions

1. How would you handle this matter? Would you inform McIverson, the school principal? Why or why not?
2. If you would not, are you not, in effect, an accomplice to an act of theft?
3. What procedures might a school district implement to curtail theft of the public's property by a few employees, while still treating the vast majority of its staff as honest people?
4. Are Tom Wicks's personal motives relevant to informing his superior of Fred's actions? If so, how?

CASE #7: AN OFFICE AFFAIR

Susan Matheson wasn't sure when her feelings about Bill had become something more than professional. Perhaps it was when she observed him for the first time in his classroom. He was simply a superb teacher. That was obvious.

It wasn't just that his lessons were carefully wrought and thoughtfully present-ed. They were also served up with a charm and wit that captivated his students. He was somehow able to appear at one with his class, a first among equals, and simultaneously to be the acknowledged authority and leader of a very difficult group of students.

Perhaps it had happened even earlier, when he had interviewed for the position at Lublow Junior High. Susan had been impressed with his boyish, fresh-out-of-college eagerness and his patent commitment to serving poor and minority pupils.

Regardless of when her feelings had changed, it was obvious now that they had. Now, not only Bill's pupils loved him. Susan did, too.

For his part, Bill had been slow to respond. Later, he had confessed to Susan that he thought that the signs of her attraction to him were figments of his imagination. How could an accomplished and very proper professional woman, especially such an attractive one, find him appealing? He had also been slow to react even after he recognized Susan's actions for what they were. After all, she was his boss. Getting sexually involved with your principal perhaps was not a good idea for a brand-new teacher.

For her part, Susan had resisted strenuously her growing attraction to Bill. It wasn't just that she was his principal, with all that that implied for their professional association. There was the matter of the rest of her staff. Were it to become known that she and Bill were having an affair, her relationship with her faculty would surely be damaged. Finally, there was the matter of her own family. While her marriage had been troubled for a long time, she had no intention of dissolving it.

Susan was under no illusions about the permanence of her affair. She knew that eventually it would end. But in the meantime, her life had been transformed. It was infused with a kind of enchantment she hadn't felt in years and might never feel again. Why should she give that up? Further, the salutary effects of the affair were not simply personal. She looked forward to each day at work with a new enthusiasm that was beginning to show in the operation of the school itself. Lublow Junior High was humming in a way that it had not in years. Surely that was a good thing.

Some Questions

1. People—both married and unmarried—have affairs all the time. Is there anything about an affair between educators that makes it more problematic than most others?
2. Superiors and subordinates also have affairs all the time. Is there anything about such a relationship between principal and teacher that makes it espe-cially problematic?
3. Suppose it is true that Bill is a superb teacher and that Lublow Junior High

is actually running better because of its principal's dalliance. If you were Susan Matheson, how would you handle this situation?

CASE #8: SOCIETAL AND INDIVIDUAL GOOD

It had had the worst reputation in the city. Nestor High suffered from a 60% dropout rate, open drug trafficking, student violence, vandalism, and the lowest achievement scores in the state. When Emanuel Diaz had arrived as principal just five years ago, no one thought he could turn the place around. Mr. Diaz started with the community. He went to the local merchants, owners of small businesses, and local factories. They all agreed with him that something had to be done for the neighborhood. Amazingly, Mr. Diaz convinced them that they were the key. He arranged enough work-study opportunities so that any student who wanted one could almost pick his or her occupational "experiment." Teachers soon joined in the cause and linked their teaching as much as possible to the work experiences students were having. Practical math and science, history of technology and labor, literature of workers, and all sorts of other "applied" aspects of the school subjects were being taught. And it was like a communicable disease. Students infected with good experiences at work and school spread their enthusiasm to others, and Mr. Diaz worked hard to make sure his "clinic" had spaces for the new patients.

And now Nestor High was among the best urban schools in the state as measured by reading scores, dropout rate, vandalism, crime, drug abuse, and subjective assessments of "atmosphere."

There was one problem, however; the few students from Nestor who applied to highly selective colleges were being turned down. Admissions officers claimed that the courses at Nestor were not academic enough and that the experience was too narrowly vocational to really prepare people for college. Mr. Diaz wondered if he had really done good for his school and its students, or if he had merely created a social salvage machine that could produce workers but not provide opportunity for true upward mobility and individual fulfillment.

Some Questions

1. Is the societal good created by Mr. Diaz's changes at Nestor in conflict with individual good? Is there an ethical issue here?
2. Are the school's primary obligations to society or to the individual? What is the nature of these obligations? Contractual? Legal? Constitutional? Traditional? Ethical? Discuss.

CASE #9: JOB REFERENCES FOR STUDENTS

In the large system in which Mrs. Goode had trained as assistant principal, school counselors handled all local calls for outside references. But here in the Bush Hills Consolidated School District, it fell to her as part of her job as principal to respond to requests from prospective local employers of students. It was a little difficult at first, because she didn't know the students too well. Still, discreet conversations with a student's teachers usually provided Mrs. Goode with enough information to satisfy her sense of a real and useful appraisal — something "canned" recommendations too often failed to provide. She felt she had an obligation to provide prospective employers with an honest appraisal of a student's job-related characteristics and his or her school record. After all, this was a public school and should serve the public.

Then she got the call from the electricians union. They needed a reference for Fred Fredricks. He had applied to become an apprentice. Mrs. Goode said she would call back, but already she knew she had a problem. Fred was probably the most notorious senior at Bush Hills. He bullied the young kids. He cut classes. He didn't do his homework. He was always being sent to the principal's office for some infraction of school rules. And he wasn't too bright.

On the other hand, she had gathered some first-hand information on his background that mitigated the situation. His mother was an alcoholic and on welfare. His father had abused Fred and currently was serving a term in jail for housebreaking. Fred had had little care growing up and had rebelled against his family. All through the years before Mrs. Goode had come to Bush Hills, the teachers had tried to help him overcome his antisocial behavior and at least learn enough to pass each grade. They knew he needed help. In fact, it looked like he would even graduate, albeit with the absolutely lowest average anyone had ever had in the history of the school.

If Mrs. Goode told the union of his grades, his absentee record, and his lack of application to school work, she knew they would turn him down. But this might be Fred's only chance to make something of his life, to become a responsible adult. She was leaning toward giving a "canned," noncommittal recommendation until she remembered that just last week there had been a story in the paper about a house that had burned down because a careless worker had crossed wires when installing a switch.

In one last, desperate effort to find a legitimate basis for helping Fred, she went to his shop teacher, only to find that Fred wasn't too handy with tools either, was sloppy finishing up work, and tended to cut corners.

Some Questions

1. What would you do if you were Mrs. Goode? How would you justify your decision?

2. Should schools serve as society's sorter? Does the school have an obligation to respond to requests for information about students? Are there any limits?

CASE #10: CONFIDENTIALITY, OBLIGATIONS, AND FRIENDSHIP

Henry Hendricks had made it a point to get to know the staff at his school personally. He remembered the warnings of his professors of school administration that if proper professional distance were not maintained, subjective personal feelings would enter into what should be impersonal, objective, professional decisions.

But Henry had always been a gregarious type; his style of leadership was personal, and it worked. He had been at Grover Cleveland High for only five years, but it was a changed place. Faculty morale was high, and an atmosphere of good, warm feelings pervaded the halls. The faculty liked him, and they worked hard.

All this went through Henry's mind as he sat across the desk from Jim Austin, the head of Cleveland's physical education department, who had asked for a confidential meeting with Henry. He and Jim had become good friends as early morning jogging companions. Henry couldn't figure out why Jim hadn't just talked to him that morning about whatever was on his mind. Jim didn't take long to get to the point now, however. First, he made it clear that this was to be a confidential talk, that if he hadn't come to respect Henry as a friend as well as a principal, he wouldn't be here. He had just found he had AIDS and wanted to stay at his job without anyone's knowing for as long as he could.

Henry's first thought was that he wished the board had a policy on AIDS; then he felt embarrassed for thinking first of himself and a way out rather than of Jim's grappling with his death notice.

Henry's next inclination was to respond to Jim as his friend and tell him he would keep his secret and let him stay on. But then Henry wondered about his obligations to his students and staff. Jim was a physical education instructor, and things might happen that would allow the virus to be spread. He wished he knew more about AIDS, but this was a little late to get an education. He needed to make a decision.

Some Questions

1. If you were Henry, what would you decide? How would you justify your decision? Did the nature of the disease influence your decision?
2. Are personal relations and any degree of friendship between administrators and staff best avoided? Discuss.

CASE #11: LOYALTY

It had taken many years of hard work and team effort. Nancy Reilly had risen through the ranks in the Milford school system with the help of many colleagues to become the first female superintendent of schools in the county. She was proud of her accomplishment, but she also knew that overcoming the sex barrier in this town required the support of many unsung heroes (and heroines) working behind the scenes over many years. Now Nancy could repay all that effort, encouragement, and trust by being the best superintendent the Milford schools ever had. It might take a few years, but she knew that she had the support of the teachers and of the parents' Coalition for Better Schools and that all would turn out well because she was dedicated to the task, as all her supporters knew. At least that's what she and they thought until "the offer" came along. It seemed that the majority party in the state felt that the only way they could win the next gubernatorial election was finally to face the charge of antifeminism by putting a woman high up in the administration. The job of Commissioner of Education was opening up and they had heard of the talent and dedication of Nancy Reilly, first female superintendent in Milford. She was just right for the job; the timing and publicity were perfect.

They contacted Nancy and offered her the position. She was torn between loyalty to Milford and to the feminist cause, not to mention her own ambition. She would have to think about it, she told them.

Some Questions

1. What would you do if you were Nancy? Is loyalty a *moral* virtue or just a personal disposition?
2. Are contracts made to be broken? Doesn't an individual have a right to advance his or her own career?

Annotated Bibliography

Aristotle. *Nicomachean Ethics*. Translated by W. D. Ross. New York: Oxford University Press, 1980.
  An important classical text on the nature of the virtues.

Arkes, Hadley. *The Philosopher in the City*. Princeton, NJ: Princeton University Press, 1981.
  An excellent treatment of ethical issues that arise in urban politics. Contains a section on education.

Baier, Kurt. *The Moral Point of View*. New York: Random House, 1965.
  Treats individual and social rules of reason and how they affect moral judgment.

Beck, Robert N., and Orr, John B. *Ethical Choice: A Case Study Approach*. New York: Free Press, 1970.
  The writings of classical and modern ethicists are excerpted and applied to contemporary problems.

Bok, Sissela. *Lying: Moral Choice in Public and Private Life*. New York: Vintage, 1979.
  Addresses the possible justifications and consequences of withholding the truth.

Bok, Sissela. *Secrets*. New York: Pantheon, 1982.
  Discusses the right and obligation to keep secrets and those situations in which keeping secrets may not be justified.

Brennan, Joseph Gerard. *Ethics and Morals*. New York: Harper & Row, 1973.
  A very readable treatment of classical and contemporary ethical theories and a consideration of such topics as morality and sex, love, death, and war and the state.

Dewey, John. *Reconstruction in Philosophy*. Boston: Beacon Press, 1957.
  A good description of Dewey's views on science and philosophy, together with his views on the application of the scientific method to ethical problems.

Dworkin, Ronald. *Taking Rights Seriously*. Cambridge, MA: Harvard University Press, 1977.
  A discussion of legal and ethical philosophy, with a good chapter on affirmative action.

Gilligan, Carol. *In A Different Voice*. Cambridge, MA: Harvard University Press, 1982.
  A feminist critique and alternative to current views on moral education.

Girvetz, Harry K. *Beyond Right and Wrong*. New York: Free Press, 1973.
A thorough treatment of ethical skepticism and an argument for "objective relativism" in ethics.

Haller, Emil J., and Strike, Kenneth A. *An Introduction to Educational Administration: Social, Legal and Ethical Perspectives*. New York: Longman, 1986.
An extensive treatment of common administrative problems from three different perspectives.

Hare, R. M. *Applications of Moral Philosophy*. Berkeley: University of California Press, 1972.
A lucid treatment of many moral concerns, including such things as relativism, the moral development of adolescents, the morality of governmental acts, and peace; deals with such questions as "What is life?" and "Can I be blamed for following orders?"

Hodgkinson, Christopher. *Towards a Philosophy of Administration*. New York: St. Martin's Press, 1978.
A treatment of a variety of philosophic issues, including ethical ones, as they apply to educational administration.

Hume, David. *A Treatise of Human Nature*. Reprinted from the original edition (first edition, 1888) in three volumes. Oxford, England: Oxford University Press, 1967.
A classic and comprehensive statement by the quintessential empiricist on matters of epistemology, human nature, and ethics.

Kant, Immanuel. *Critique of Practical Reason*. Translated by Lewis W. Beck. Indianapolis, IN: Bobbs-Merrill, 1956.
The classical statement and defense of a nonconsequentialist ethical position. Hard reading, but worthwhile.

Kimbrough, Ralph B. *Ethics*. Arlington, VA: American Association of School Administrators, 1985.
A brief treatment of central topics in educational administration.

Levine, Alan H., and Cary, Eve. *The Rights of Students*. New York: Discus, 1977.
An American Civil Liberties Union handbook on constitutional rights.

MacIntyre, Alisdair. *After Virtue*. South Bend, IN: University of Notre Dame Press, 1982.
A recent influential critique of modern ethical theories and a defense of an Aristotelian viewpoint.

Mill, John Stuart. *On Liberty*. Indianapolis, IN: Bobbs-Merrill, 1956.
The classic arguments for freedom of opinion and lifestyle.

Mill, John Stuart. "Utilitarianism." In Bentham, Jeremy, and Mill, John Stuart, *The Utilitarians*. Garden City, NY: Academic Press, Doubleday, 1973.
An excellent and brief statement of utilitarianism.

Noddings, Nell. *Caring: A Feminine Approach to Ethics and Moral Education*. Berkeley: University of California Press, 1984.
A femininist approach to ethics and moral education.

Peters, Richard S. *Ethics and Education*. London: George Allen & Unwin, 1970.
A discussion of several ethical concepts, such as punishment, respect for persons, freedom, and equality, in an educational context.

Rawls, John. *A Theory of Justice*. Cambridge, MA: Harvard University Press, 1971.
Possibly the best contemporary statement of a liberal theory of social justice.

Rich, John Martin. *Professional Ethics in Education*. Springfield, Il.: Charles C. Thomas, Publisher, 1984.
Deals with various issues in professional ethics. Thoroughly researched. A good place to begin research on a variety of topics.

Robinson, George M., and Moulton, Janice. *Ethical Problems in Higher Education*. Englewood Cliffs, NJ: Prentice-Hall, 1985.
An excellent treatment of central ethical issues in higher education.

Rubin, David. *The Rights of Teachers*. New York: Discus, 1971.
An American Civil Liberties Union handbook on constitutional rights.

Shaver, James P., and Strong, William. *Facing Value Decisions*. 2nd ed. New York: Teachers College Press, 1982.
Explores values education within a democratic context and the rational foundations of values.

Sola, Peter Andre, ed. *Ethics, Education and Administrative Decisions*. New York: Peter Lang, 1984.
A collection of papers on a variety of issues concerning administrative ethics.

Strike, Kenneth. *Educational Policy and the Just Society*. Urbana: University of Illinois Press, 1982.
A discussion of the concepts of liberty, equality, and rationality as applied to a range of educational problems.

Strike, Kenneth. *Liberty and Learning*. New York: St. Martin's Press, 1982.
Develops a theory of liberty for education. Contains chapters on academic freedom and students' rights.

Strike, Kenneth A. and Soltis, Jonas F. *The Ethics of Teaching*. Thinking About Education Series. New York: Teachers College Press, 1985.
A book, similar in purpose and organization to *The Ethics of School Administration*, but focused on ethical issues in teaching.

Toulmin, Stephen. *Reason in Ethics*. Cambridge, England: Cambridge University Press, 1970.
Contrasts different ethical theories and points to a parallel between common sense and ethical reasoning.

Index